Beyond the Traditional Essay

Increasing Student Agency in a Diverse Classroom with Nondisposable Assignments

Edited by

Melissa Ryan
Alfred University

Kerry Kautzman
Alfred University

Series in Education

VERNON PRESS

Copyright © 2022 by the authors.

All rights reserved. No part of this publication may be reproduced, stored in a retrieval system, or transmitted in any form or by any means, electronic, mechanical, photocopying, recording, or otherwise, without the prior permission of Vernon Art and Science Inc.
www.vernonpress.com

In the Americas:
Vernon Press
1000 N West Street, Suite 1200,
Wilmington, Delaware 19801
United States

In the rest of the world:
Vernon Press
C/Sancti Espiritu 17,
Malaga, 29006
Spain

Series in Education

Library of Congress Control Number: 2022931470

ISBN: 978-1-64889-489-3

Also available: 978-1-64889-408-4 [Hardback]; 978-1-64889-430-5 [PDF, E-Book]

Product and company names mentioned in this work are the trademarks of their respective owners. While every care has been taken in preparing this work, neither the authors nor Vernon Art and Science Inc. may be held responsible for any loss or damage caused or alleged to be caused directly or indirectly by the information contained in it.

Every effort has been made to trace all copyright holders, but if any have been inadvertently overlooked the publisher will be pleased to include any necessary credits in any subsequent reprint or edition.

Cover design by Vernon Press using elements designed by pch.vector / Freepik.

Table of Contents

List of Figures v

Introduction vii
Kerry Kautzman
Alfred University

Melissa Ryan
Alfred University

Chapter 1
A Model of Relational Learning and Knowledge Production: Using Podcasts in a Writing Intensive Native American/Indigenous Literatures Course 1
Francisco D. Delgado
Borough of Manhattan Community College, CUNY

Chapter 2
Adding to Archives, Stories, and Conversations: Dramaturgy, Collaboration, and the Non-terminating Essay Assignment 17
Aoise Stratford
Cornell University

Chapter 3
Comparative Reading by Students in the World: For Promoting Better Understanding of Literature and Peace in the World 33
Akiyoshi Suzuki
Nagasaki University, Japan

Chapter 4
DEI, NDAs, and the Value of Literature: Dismantling Educational Privilege with Nontraditional Assignments 53
Melissa Ryan
Alfred University

Chapter 5
Renewable Assignments, from Paper to Trees   71
Allison M. Cummings
Southern New Hampshire University

Chapter 6
Renewable Assignments and the Integrity of Intellectual Work   89
James M. Skidmore
University of Waterloo

Chapter 7
Learning Outcomes of Non-disposable Assignments: An Approach to Measuring the Results   107
Kerry Kautzman
Alfred University

Contributors   123

Index   125

List of Figures

Figure 6.1: Criteria Distinguishing Different Kinds of Assignments — 93
Figure 6.2: The 5Rs — 95
Figure 6.3: The CC Licences & The 5R Activities — 96
Figure 6.4: Relationship between OER and Creative Commons licenses — 96

Introduction

Kerry Kautzman

Alfred University

Melissa Ryan

Alfred University

Literature classes often follow what seems like an inevitable arc toward a thesis-driven literary analysis essay. But while it's certainly true that being able to make evidence-based analytical arguments is a fundamental exercise of critical thinking skills, this collection explores other –perhaps more engaging – ways to demonstrate those skills, using tools and forms that transcend academic boundaries. Instead of what open pedagogy advocate David Wiley terms "disposable assignments" – written only for the instructor to grade, and then tossed away and forgotten ("What Is Open Pedagogy?") – the scholars collected here discuss a wide range of assignments that contribute to public knowledge: work that is shared across networks of learning, that *does* something, that isn't just for a teacher's grade.

For many of us, the value of what we do is self-evident – but we recognize that the value of the humanities in general, or literature in particular, is not necessarily self-evident to others, whether colleagues across campus or society at large. As the precipitous decline in humanities majors over the last decade suggests, literary study in an outcomes-focused society is, like the assignments Wiley targets, seen as eminently disposable. Liberal arts advocates spreading the word in the popular press consistently demonstrate that the value differential is a matter of perception; yes, engineers outearn English majors, but on the whole, the earnings differences between the seemingly practical STEM majors and the dilettantish humanities are not significant. What matters, as Benjamin Schmidt writes in the *Atlantic*, is that since the financial crisis of 2008, students have learned to think that they *should* want a STEM degree, in what he characterizes as "a largely misguided effort to enhance their chances on the job market" ("The Humanities Are In Crisis").[1] Faculty may know that

---

[1] For evidence of the decline in humanities majors, the National Center for Education Statistics offers this table recording degrees conferred by major: https://nces.ed.gov/programs/digest/d20/tables/dt20_322.10.asp. For related data and interpretation, see Schmidt, "The Humanities Are In Crisis."

literature courses strengthen core skills in critical thinking and communication, but outside of our hallways English seminars are seen as cloistered and arcane, or narrow in their postgraduate applicability; the core professional skills developed in the writing of five pages on a line of Dickinson poetry are not universally clear. In short, traditional, disposable assignments don't necessarily make our value visible, even – or perhaps especially – to the student completing them.

One response to our relevance crisis is to rethink assignments in a way that students might find more vital and engaging. Innovative assignments may productively disrupt the routine, giving students a fresh perspective just by asking them to put materials together in a different way. For example, instead of asking for a formulaic comparison-contrast essay, instructors might have students write the introduction to a hypothetical anthology putting multiple texts in dialogue. Or, instead of analyzing a legal case, an assignment might have students pretend they're judges applying a precedent in making a decision. Assignments like these – of which there are many examples online, shared both by individual instructors and at the institutional level through Teaching & Learning Centers – are more engaging because they give students a more active role, and they may actually address core objectives even more directly than a traditional essay with its tired structure can. But they're also pretend. They defer the real value until later (when I actually become a judge, when I actually become an editor). Really moving beyond disposable assignments means not just simulating the way writing works in the world, but engaging in the real thing: creating public resources and participating in the learning of others.

This emphasis on nondisposability – on what are known as "renewable" assignments – emerges from the Open Pedagogy movement and related interest in Open Educational Resources and OER-enabled pedagogy, all of which resist the limitations on learning embedded in the model of intellectual production as commercial product. Traditional assignments are organized around the closely related concepts of privacy and property. The assignment is a private transaction between teacher and student, taking place primarily in the margins of the paper (like the private space of the office hour), and the results are a closely kept (FERPA-protected) secret. This intellectual production is then a product, the student's private property (students are consistently surprised to learn that they can, in effect, steal from themselves by plagiarizing their own work). In contrast to this pedagogy of private property, renewable assignments see learning as public in both senses: something that happens in the open, for the general welfare.

Open pedagogy fosters a reexamination of how we learn and what we can do with the artifacts of learning. Open Educational Resources (OERs) in any medium are defined by open licensing, usually through Creative Commons licenses, and are characterized by the 5 Rs: materials in this category can be reused, retained, redistributed, revised, and remixed. As its name implies, OER-enabled pedagogy uses OERs and their 5R permissions to achieve the goals of open pedagogy. All of the media transformed by open pedagogy and OER-enabled pedagogy (books, lessons, videos, podcasts, websites, audio-visual materials) result from the technological, digital advancements that allow students and faculty to learn by doing as well as by what others do, without the limits of geography or time. OER-enabled pedagogy addresses four outcomes proposed by Wiley and Hilton as a test that serves to eliminate materials that claim to be open pedagogy when in practice the materials are privately licensed. First, students create new artifacts or revise/remix existing OER. Because students can both (#2) publicly share the materials and (#3) openly license them, the remixed or newly created artifact adds value to the world and therefore passes the fourth test by not only supporting the learning of its author (Wiley and Hilton 137).

Open Pedagogy is more broadly defined not just by licensing but by ideology, by its ethics of collaboration and accessibility. It issues both practical and theoretical challenges to the traditional classroom model – that is, the model that imposes cost prohibitions on learning and assumes a hierarchy from teacher as agent-expert to student as passive consumer of educational content. In so doing, this approach reconceptualizes institutional power dynamics in ways that make meaningful education more available to all students: "Knowledge consumption and knowledge creation are not separate but parallel processes, as knowledge is co-constructed, contextualized, cumulative, iterative, and recursive. In this way, Open Pedagogy invites us to focus on how we can increase access to higher education and how we can increase access to knowledge–both its reception and its creation" (DeRosa and Jhangiani). Thinking from an open pedagogical perspective means re-seeing the goals and structures of educational institutions in a way that recognizes student agency.

With its emphasis on equity and inclusivity, Open Pedagogy overlaps with another relatively recent pedagogical development: Universal Design for Learning (UDL), which seeks to create a flexible learning environment in which students with learning differences can thrive. UDL is a framework governing course design that seeks to maximize the value of the curriculum for diverse learners. Instead of normalizing a certain student population (nondisabled, nonmarginalized) and providing accommodations for others, UDL recognizes that thoughtful course design removes barriers to learning for all students. An accommodation like a sidewalk cutout may increase access for a person in a wheelchair, but it's also useful for someone pushing a stroller or someone riding a bike. In an educational context, students with documented learning disabilities might be allowed extra time on an exam as an accommodation, but a UDL perspective might instead ask whether a timed exam is the best or only way for students to demonstrate their learning.

Based on extensive research in the science of learning, the UDL guidelines follow three core principles. First, they remind educators to "provide multiple means of representation." Instructors can reach diverse students – those with sensory or cognitive disabilities, or second language learners, or just those with different processing strengths – by providing information in multiple forms (audio, visual, textual, supplemental context, etc.). The second principle is to "provide multiple means of action and expression"; that is, to be mindful of the way diverse learners will interact with physical and digital tools, to support students in their planning and self-monitoring, and give them multiple ways to demonstrate what they know. And finally, UDL guidelines encourage instructors to "provide multiple means of engagement." What might motivate one student will cause another to shut down, so instructors should devise a range of strategies for generating interest, enthusiasm, and a sense of self-efficacy – that is, for activating the affective dimensions of learning (CAST).

The goals articulated in these guidelines and the measures CAST offers for evaluating course design dovetail with the aims and purposes of nondisposable assignments. For example, Checkpoint 7.2 in the CAST rubric for Engagement, "Optimize relevance, value, and authenticity," reinforces the objectives we encounter in this volume: class work should be "personalized and contextualized to learners' lives," "culturally relevant and responsive," and "socially relevant," and instructors should "design activities so that learning outcomes are authentic, communicate to real audiences, and reflect a purpose that is clear to the participants." Similarly, Checkpoint 5.1: "Use multiple media for communication," a way of eliminating barriers to Action and Expression, is central to several of the projects described in the essays collected here; having students create podcasts or video presentations, for example, puts this principle into practice. As the UDL guidelines point out, fluency in a variety of media is useful for all students: "It is important for all learners to learn composition, not just writing, and to learn the optimal medium for any particular content of expression and audience." In other words, a student whose ADD has produced debilitating writing anxiety may benefit from an option to record an idea verbally rather than in writing, but so would a student who will need to present ideas verbally in professional life.

UDL guidelines, like nondisposable assignments, invite us as educators to examine our learning goals and think more broadly about how students could achieve them, rather than assigning tasks because those are the tasks that were assigned to us (or because those are the things we're good at). They seek to separate the means from the ends, so that we can get beyond the idea that a

Introduction   xi

literary analysis essay is the only way to demonstrate literary analysis. And both open pedagogy and UDL seek to remove artificial barriers – restrictive licenses or restrictive course design – that limit access to education.

In other words, the pedagogical context for the essays that follow revolves around empowering students – giving them the agency to build and collaborate rather than absorb and regurgitate. For Francisco Delgado, this takes the form of having students create podcasts as an optional alternative to the traditional researched essay in a Writing Intensive Native American/Indigenous Literatures course. Breaking down the steps of podcast production as parallel to and overlapping with the conventional writing process, Delgado draws connections between the thematic work of the course – what it means to live relationally – and the collaborative ethos of this project. Instead of working in isolation (or in competition), students forged relationships through this podcast assignment. They worked as a class to develop a rubric, and they transformed the traditional univocal argument into a set of ideas advanced through discussion, making this nondisposable assignment one way to "truly decolonize the classroom."

Aoise Stratford also emphasizes the productive potential of building connections in "Adding to Archives, Stories, and Conversations: Dramaturgy, Collaboration, and the Non-terminating Essay Assignment." Writing from the perspective of a playwright and dramaturg and offering collaborative techniques borrowed from theatre, Stratford details three easily adapted assignments for increasing student agency and engagement. One assignment invites students to participate in the making of the syllabus; another asks for a creative response to a work they've explored together; and a third functions as a dramaturg's casebook, a collaboratively developed collection of resources. Entering into these larger academic conversations, as Stratford shows, individual students produce work that contributes "ongoing pedagogical value for all the learners in the class (including the instructor)."

For Akiyoshi Suzuki, the collaborative framework is even more far-reaching. Offering a wealth of examples to illustrate how literature defies attempts to neatly categorize East and West, Suzuki proposes strategies for building international interpretive partnerships. A joint class of Anglophone and Asian learners might explore connections between Anglophone modernism of the twentieth century and tenth- and eleventh-century Japanese literature; or such a class could discover both cultural affinities and differences reading a classic Anglophone text like *The Great Gatsby* from Eastern and Western vantage points. As Suzuki demonstrates, online resources facilitate projects that foster a deeper understanding of cultural Others.

Melissa Ryan describes another kind of web resource that also seeks to develop cultural competence. She articulates concerns about the relationship between traditional literary analysis assignments and educational privilege, seeing disposable assignments as in some cases more than a missed opportunity. Reflecting on the capacity of nondisposable assignments to address diversity, equity, and inclusion goals, as well as to make the value of literature more available to all students, she shares lessons learned from some preliminary steps toward rethinking literature assignments.

Allison Cummings considers the topic of nondisposable assignments from the perspective of renewable (human) resources in "Renewable Assignments, From Paper to Trees." Mapping tools have inspired a range of innovative projects for building ecological literacy; her survey of the field, grounded in pedagogical scholarship around what makes assignments meaningful, describes projects in the Environmental Humanities that foster "an ethic of connection to community or planet." Her digital Nature Log assignment, for example, pins student contributions to google maps, resulting in a public multimedia story of place; similarly, a video project gives students an opportunity to "read" landscape in a way that generates questions about land use. But at the same time, Cummings is realistic in her view of what such public-facing assignments actually do, and she offers a moving defense of private writing that creators – like her own great grandmother – could have disposed of but chose not to.

James Skidmore also questions whether all writing should be made public in the sense defined by OER advocates. Open licensing may raise questions about protecting the integrity of student work – and in experimenting with renewable assignments in his course titled "Truth – Reconciliation – Story," he found that students weren't ready for all he was asking them to do. However, to get students to engage with content dealing with human rights abuses, it's necessary to minimize the "transactional" element so that students don't see it as just another requirement on the way to a degree, and rethinking the usual essay (the disposable "receipt" in the work-for-grades transaction) plays a crucial role in this process. Skidmore describes modifying the renewable assignment to balance idealistic goals with the realities of the semester while shifting the focus from product to process.

One of the challenges with nontraditional assignments is, in fact, determining how successful they are. While we may intuitively or anecdotally recognize increased engagement, Kerry Kautzman in "Learning Outcomes of Renewable Assignments" demonstrates an approach to measuring the results. She focuses on two different kinds of renewable assignments: a critical edition to be submitted to an OER anthology of literature offering in-depth study of a canonical text and its socio-historical context, and a blog created by international-domestic student pairs exploring the developing of intercultural competency. Both assignments are writing-intensive, collaborative, multi-step projects, and both result in a digital product available both for the students' own future use and for assessment purposes. Kautzman models how to analyze the effectiveness of these assignments using rubrics that describe learning outcomes associated with traditional disposable assignments.

Taken together, these essays offer both scholarly context and practical advice, both the thoughtful rationale for going beyond the traditional essay and lessons learned from a wide range of pedagogical experiments. They gesture toward the possibilities of our digital present, in which enhanced technologies of communication and expression meet our sharpened awareness of what higher education can do, and for whom.

Bibliography

CAST. Universal Design for Learning Guidelines version 2.2., 2018, https://udlguidelines.cast.org/. Accessed 6 June 2021.

DeRosa, Robin and Rajiv Jhangiani. "Open Pedagogy." *Open Pedagogy Notebook*, http://openpedagogy.org/open-pedagogy. Accessed 15 July 2021.

Schmidt, Benjamin. "The Humanities Are In Crisis." *The Atlantic*, 23 August 2018, https://www.theatlantic.com/ideas/archive/2018/08/the-humanities-face-a-crisisof-confidence/567565/

Wiley, David. "What Is Open Pedagogy?" Open Content, 21 October 2013, https://opencontent.org/blog/archives/2975.

Wiley, David and John Levi Hilton III. "Defining OER-Enabled Pedagogy." *International Review of Research in Open and Distributed Learning*, vol. 19, no. 4, September 2018, p. 133-147, DOI: https://doi.org/10.19173/irrodl.v19i4.3601.

Chapter 1

A Model of Relational Learning and Knowledge Production: Using Podcasts in a Writing Intensive Native American/Indigenous Literatures Course

Francisco D. Delgado
Borough of Manhattan Community College, CUNY

Abstract

In "A Model of Relational Learning and Knowledge Production: Using Podcasts in a Writing Intensive Native American/Indigenous Literatures Course," Francisco Delgado (Borough of Manhattan Community College, CUNY) explores the benefits of having students create their own podcasts: students developed their analytical reading and writing skills while engaging a public outside of the classroom and connecting with the course material in a way that increased student ownership of and pride in their work. Drawing on scholarship on cultural sustaining pedagogies, Delgado demonstrates how the podcast assignment showed students the value of being able to produce knowledge in a variety of mediums and contexts while also fulfilling university learning outcomes tied to communication skills, humanistic critique, information & technology literacy, and multicultural awareness and social responsibility.

Keywords: podcasts, Native American/Indigenous literature, educational technology, collaborative assignments, open pedagogy

***

Introduction

This paper, and the podcast assignment it describes, originates from an Open Education Resource (OER)/Zero Textbook Cost (ZTC) workshop held on June 4 and 11, 2019, at my home institution, the Borough of Manhattan Community College (CUNY). It was at this two-day workshop, designed to help faculty from across the disciplines develop their courses using no-cost materials, where I started seriously considering using podcasts not only as assigned texts but as an option for the final project.

Podcasts are not new to the college classroom, however. They have become the focus of a growing body of scholarship (much of it, appropriately enough, publicly available) and even write-ups in academic publications like *Chronicle* and *Inside Higher Ed*, as well as in more generalist publications like *The Atlantic*, *The New York Times*, and *NPR*. Alix Mammina points out that teachers have been integrating podcasts, and podcasting, into curricula for more than a decade ("Teaching the Art of Listening"). And just as long as teachers have used podcasts, they have felt anxious about doing so, fearing that podcasts are not as rigorous as traditional writing assignments like the research essay. Rick Cole and Beth Kramer assuage these anxieties when they point out, citing colleagues who use the *Serial* podcast in their classroom, that podcasts "le[ad] to an increase in reading and critical thinking, with students spending more time analyzing material like clues and maps, writing in journals, and reading transcripts, blogs, and reports" ("Podcasts and the Twenty-First Century"). A possible explanation for this anxiety about assigning podcasts might relate to its novelty as a college-level assignment. But what Cole's and Kramer's argument shows, similar to my own experiences, is that students often embrace the challenges presented by podcasts. Furthermore, rather than viewing podcasts as easier than traditional reading and writing assignments, students understand them as the unique challenges they are, which I will discuss in greater detail in the following sections.

The context of this essay is my Fall 2019 class on Native American/Indigenous Literatures, a body of work that no student in class was familiar with. Additionally, none of them identified as Native American/Indigenous peoples – at least in the context of North America and the Pacific, which was the geographical scope of the course. The course was also an upper-level Writing Intensive (WI) course. As Writing Intensive, the course was designed to prompt students to produce a minimum of twelve pages of revised writing by the end of the semester, and more importantly, be instructed through the writing process in a deliberate, step-by-step manner. Participation in the *process* of writing, in other words, received a greater emphasis than in a usual college-level class. For instance, the preliminary assignments of the Podcast sequence accounted for a total of 30% of the overall class grade (10% for the Podcast Overview, 10% for a revised Overview and explanation of the First Talking Point, and another 10% for an in-class presentation), in contrast to the 20% placed on the finished podcast. These assignments will be explained in greater detail in the third section of this essay. This emphasis on process, however, is a longstanding tenet of Composition Studies scholarship. Heidi Estrem, for instance, explains, "Understanding and identifying how writing is in itself an act of thinking can help people more intentionally recognize and engage with writing as a creative activity, inextricably linked to thought" (19). To add to this, the writing process in place for this course highlights how "thought" can change from one piece of writing to the next. The sequence thus demonstrated for students how their thinking on their podcast topic evolved – and that this type of inconsistency is actually natural and productive. University requirements dictate that, in order to graduate, students must pass at least one WI course, and by their own admission, students enrolled in this course strictly to fulfill this graduation requirement. They were in no way influenced by the topic when they registered. The students were also in their final, or second-to-last, semester. While this speaks to the students' motivations for enrolling in the course (it was a graduation requirement), this reality also reflects their considerable writing abilities. They had already completed the first-year writing sequence (English Composition followed by Introduction to Literature). This course was thus likely the students' final course in which critical reading, writing, and listening skills would be emphasized. These same skills were identified in the course learning outcomes and, as I will explain in the sections that follow, fulfilled in the lead-up of the podcast final project.

Becoming Familiar with Podcasts

If I hoped for students to choose to make their own podcast for their final project, I needed to expose them to the genre early on. I gave students the option to create their own podcasts for their final project because I wanted them to have more than one option to express their knowledge. I wanted to give students an alternative to the research essay, as well, because of the predominant attitude that it is of limited use – or, to quote Composition Studies scholars, a "disposable assignment." David Wiley has explained that disposable assignments "add no value to the world [and] suck value out of the world" ("Open Pedagogy"). I was hoping the option of a podcast, a medium of growing popularity outside the confines of a college classroom, would prompt students to realize that their work can, and should, reach beyond the scope of our fifteen-week course.

But first, students needed to feel as if they understood the format of podcasts if they were to feel confident enough to create one of their own. As Charles Bazerman explains, "Genre recognition provides a necessary clue for locating and making sense of any piece of paper or any digital display that comes before our eyes" (36). Before students can create their own podcasts, in other words, they have to "mak[e] sense" of the structure – understanding, of course, that no podcast series is structured exactly the same. This demystifies the genre which, by their own admission, none of the students had any experience with. One of the students' first assignments was listening to the first episode of *All My Relations*, a podcast devoted to Native/Indigenous issues and hosted by Matika Wilbur and Dr. Adrienne Keene. This episode covered some key concepts for our course – concepts we would return to throughout the semester together – most notably the idea of living in good relations, or "living relationally." Following their listening to the podcast, which I prepared them to complete by giving them overhead questions about the episode's main ideas, we began our class discussions by asking students to reflect on their listening experiences. All the students who shared expressed enjoying the experience. And the main struggle for students seemed to be the ability to write down exact quotations, which prompted a review of the importance of paraphrasing. Yet, despite their struggles to take notes as deeply as they would have liked, students showed in our discussions that they could identify and analyze the main components of a podcast. They also shared that, despite what they initially thought, podcasts required their uninterrupted focus. They could not do other coursework or chores around the house while listening.

My own teaching experiences have helped me realize that these types of reflective conversations require a deliberate line of questioning. Instead of asking, for instance, "What are the features of a podcast?," a question that could be too broad in scope for students to feel comfortable answering, we began our discussion more specifically about how the podcast started. Students quickly identified that the podcasts started with the hosts identifying themselves, as well as articulating the nature of their professional work and the name(s) of their Indigenous nations: Matika Wilbur, for instance, states in the first five seconds of the podcast that she "belong[s] to the Swinomish and Tulalip people" of Washington state. Students identify the importance of Wilbur's word choice here: instead of stating that she "is" Swinomish and Tulalip – how those of us who have grown up in mainstream American culture have been taught to conceive of our identities, with language mirroring ownership – Wilbur instead describes her relationship as one of belonging. Claiming an identity can be unidirectional, whereas belonging is more mutual with two parties claiming each other. This point came up again later on in our discussion as a component of what it means to "live in good relations." Relations, like belonging, are mutual. We cannot claim a relation, simply put, that does not claim us back. And how we forge a relation with a community is by making ourselves available to them. Students demonstrated an understanding, then, that if they chose to create their own podcast later on, they would need to begin by acknowledging their positions as outsiders to the community they would be discussing.

This opening introduces listeners to the speakers and also tells us what brought them to their current work. In this way, students understood that the opening section of the podcast is very similar to an essay introduction: the hosts' introductions of themselves served as the proverbial "hook," the definition of key terms like "all my relations" situates the discussion that follows in an ongoing discourse, and the hosts conclude this section by giving us what could arguably be considered their thesis statement for the episode, in which they lay out the objectives of their podcast and the importance of relationships. Wilbur explains, "our primary identity is inextricably connected to our relationships ... that relationship to land and water is our primary way of identifying ourselves. And then of course we also see ourselves as our grandmother's granddaughters, and we see our role and responsibility and purpose directly connected to our lineage" (*Relations*). Living in good relations, then, is about understanding that no thought or action exists in isolation; that, whether or not we choose to acknowledge it, our lives are intrinsically linked to others, both humans and non-humans, and the world around us.

Identifying how the beginning of the podcast functions as an introduction, we then continued our analogy between podcasts and essays – a genre that students are much more familiar with despite what they (and we) may think – by discussing how they elaborated on the supporting points of their thesis statement. Typically, students noted, we do this in the body paragraphs, but how does the structure of the argument change when the argument is being expressed in a podcast – specifically, the episode of *All My Relations* that they had listened to and annotated in preparation for class? The separate, but linked, supporting points that students identified were the contrasting approaches to identity between Native and non-Native peoples (2:30 – 8:00) and the impact of cultural stereotypes on identity (8:00 – 13:00), which students traced to the lingering influence of colonialism as the hosts discussed it for a few minutes starting roughly at the 32:00 minute mark. Students responded to each of these supporting points by stating whether or not they agreed with the hosts' arguments and by identifying how exactly each of these points was related to what preceded it and what followed.

This exercise on identifying the key features of a podcast was necessary to develop their critical listening skills. The importance of these skills is mentioned in one of the Course Learning Outcomes, which stress the ability to "write, read, listen, and speak critically and effectively." Shannon Draucker similarly asserts that podcasts cultivate critical listening skills in students: "By listening to each other's podcasts, [students] had to get used to hearing each other's voices at length and sitting with others' ideas before they respond. These sustained listening practices gave students opportunities to encounter other ways of writing and thinking, expand their own views on music and justice movements, and form collective strategies for social change" ("Collaborative learning"). Listening to an argument is a different experience from reading one; and yet, when I sit back and reflect on my own teaching practices over the last decade, I have tended to emphasize critical reading and writing skills at the expense of critical listening skills, and this stems largely from the absence of audio recordings as assignments. The use of podcasts in this class rectified this.

With this class, knowing that it culminated in a Final Project that students could complete by working together to create their own podcasts, I was determined to change that. Introducing the podcast medium early in the semester was the first step to familiarizing students with the genre. Understanding how a podcast is structured is key to helping students feel comfortable enough to undertake the venture of creating one of their own. Paraphrasing Howard Tinberg, who argues that metacognition ("how [something] came to be") is perhaps more important than cognition, I would point out that this deeper understanding of form is perhaps more important than knowing the how-to of podcast creation ("Metacognition"). But students would still need to be guided through the how-to process of creating their podcasts and understand that it required the same type of process they already knew from their research writing experiences.

Developing their Podcasts, Reflecting on the Process

Students created their podcasts piece by piece, reflecting on their processes and the development of their ideas at each stage of the process. Part of this step-by-step approach of podcast development is designed to align with the course learning outcome requiring students to practice "the process of writing through in-class writing, revising, and workshops." Writing, even if it is not a traditional research essay, is a process that takes time and effort. It is not a static product that we produce once and move on from, and it is unfortunately not something any of us will perfect on our first attempts. Worthwhile writing, as the students and I discussed, only results once a piece has undergone the very process outlined in this learning outcome, which is only complete after a round of revisions following a workshop (and maybe not even then).

The first step in the process of students' developing their podcasts was figuring out how their finished podcasts would be evaluated. We created a rubric that was particular to the podcast medium and that took into account the audio nature of the work and placed greater emphasis on collaboration. Also, because I want students to realize their potential as knowledge producers, especially in the form of podcasts, I opted to set aside class time when the students and I would discuss this matter together. Based on the podcasts that we had listened to and discussed as a class, what were the features of a successful podcast? The first feature students identified was a clear articulation of the podcast's argument at the beginning, which is similar to where a thesis statement is located in an essay. We then reviewed how the podcasts we listened to progressed from there: how did the host, or hosts, set up their subsequent talking points? How did they move from one point to the next? In this way, students reviewed the importance of transitions and structure in their writing. Just because they opted out of the Research Essay option, in other words, would not mean that they could produce a final project devoid of structure.

Working together, we decided on the features of an "A" podcast versus the features of a "B" podcast, which, as students pointed out, although close in analytical value, was not as clear in its focus as the "A" podcast and did not execute as deep a reading as was necessary to earn an "A." A "C podcast" presents more of "a topic of discussion" than a thoughtfully rendered argument. As it begins with a "topic" instead of an argument, the "C" podcast also "rarely exceeds summary, making the host's own argument difficult to decipher." The "D" podcast is one that relies entirely on summary. Simply put, rather than offering a concise argument that is developed over a series of talking points rooted in analysis of specific passages from the primary text, the "D" podcast would function only as a reiteration of what others had already written. The emphasis in the rubric was on the content and structure of the argument and how well the hosts used evidence from the primary and secondary sources. But because the podcast was an audio project, we also had to take into account the listenability of the finished podcasts.

We chose, however, to keep the technical focus to a minimum. The class, after all, was designed to foster a greater understanding about Native/Indigenous literatures, not a greater understanding of podcast technology. But we were mindful of the fact that in order for the students' understanding of the literature to be expressed, the audibility had to be at a certain level. Beyond audible clarity, though, the students and I did not feel comfortable placing too much emphasis on any aspect of the technical proficiency. For instance, in the rubric we designed together, the "A" podcast "largely flows smoothly" – language that allows for some technical glitches to occur without any impact on the grade. The "B" podcast has "a couple of instances when the audio is difficult to hear, thus making the conversation hard to follow," and the "C" podcast shows recurring technical issues, making the podcast difficult to decipher in many instances. Our course, however, was focused on developing our critical reading, writing, thinking, and listening skills of Native American/Indigenous Literatures, not about developing any specific technical prowess. The experience of evaluating podcasts was a new venture for me – just as creating podcasts was new to them. Creating the rubric with students was facilitated by my desire for students to assume their agency as knowledge producers. They would thus not only produce a document of their knowledge with the podcast, but they would have a heavy influence on how the work would be evaluated based on our discussion of the grading guidelines.

As this was a new venture for all of the students, I understood immediately that I needed to integrate reflection activities at every stage in the process. Having students reflect on the development of their ideas at every stage would show them, by their own articulation, how much they had learned over the course of the final project sequence. As Hollis Glaser put it much more succinctly in her post, "What makes a meaningful assignment?," "reflection creates the meaning". I did not want students to simply be able to identify connections between the primary text and their secondary sources; I wanted them to understand what they were doing throughout the writing process, even if they did not understand it while they were doing it. Understanding their processes is arguably just as important as having a process in the first place. This way, the process becomes in some way replicable; and in these instances when students cannot exactly recreate the writing context and procedure they used for this specific assignment, they will have more experience problem-solving their writing processes due to their completion of the reflection assignments integrated into this process, as Cognitive Science scholarship shows. In a context more relevant to Writing Pedagogy, Victor Rivero describes the concept of "unlearning" as "a strategy to combat existing ways of thinking that may impede one's problem-solving abilities" ("Unlearning"). Problem-solving during a writing process means understanding that no two writing assignments are exactly alike – and that taking the time to reflect on what works (and what doesn't) is just as valuable as time spent writing.

This time to reflect would help them generate meaning out of their writing process that is sometimes absent when students are asked to complete a series of assignments without time to reflect on them before moving on to the next. Students identify and explain how their individual podcasts conform to the conventions of the medium, as we have discussed in class: how, for instance, does their presentation of their argument align with Keene's and Wilbur's in *All My Relations*? If it differs, how does the structure they ultimately selected help them make their own individual argument more effectively? Furthermore, in asking students to reflect on the growth of their projects as they develop, I am asking them to articulate the exact skills they are developing and the specific concepts they are exploring in their work. This is important work, especially towards the end of the semester, when, as Dana Lynn Driscoll points out, students' belief in the transfer value of their coursework begins to decrease ("Connected, Disconnected, or Uncertain"). In a course on a topic that many students do not immediately see as connected to their major field of study or future career aspirations in the first place, having them articulate the development of their skillset and multicultural understanding is a valuable exercise. For one pair of students, whose podcast I will discuss at great length in the following section, they discussed how their analysis of Louise Erdrich's 1983 novel *Love Medicine* ultimately developed their understanding of the concept "living in good relations," a foundational concept that we explored earlier in the semester and returned to throughout.

A Case Study of One Student Podcast

Of a class of twenty-five students (24 of whom submitted work for the final project), six students chose the Podcast option, meaning three pairs of two. I required students to work in pairs to emphasize collaboration, which we heard in and discussed about both of our exemplar podcasts, the aforementioned *All My Relations* and *The Cuts* hosted by Sterlin Harjo. I also wanted students to avoid producing an *InfoWars*-style podcast: one person ranting, unchallenged, because it seemed like the exact opposite of living and learning in good relations, which formed the foundation of our class discussions throughout the semester.

Podcasters began by articulating the overview of their podcast. In this preliminary assignment, they articulated the topic of their podcast, their central argument (understanding, of course, that this might change as their work on the assignment continued and that that was okay) and how exactly they planned on structuring their recording: would it be framed as a discussion, as we heard Dr. Keene and Wilbur do, as an interview, or some other form that they believed would help them develop their specific argument? Students earned full credit on these initial assignments. Then, following feedback that they received from classmates in our in-class workshop (and from me), they revised their Overviews – and added their first supporting point. In this assignment, they also closely read one passage from the text that they planned on using as their evidence and integrated a short passage from one of their secondary sources in support of their argument. In this way, the assignment mirrored the work their classmates who chose the Research Essay assignment were doing: carefully elaborating on their argument by articulating and explaining the first supporting point of their thesis statement.

Podcasters had the additional task of exploring how they would frame this supporting point *as an actual discussion*. Unlike research essay writing where this conversation seems more theoretical or abstract – taking the form of citations and responses – the discussion of the podcast between the partners would have to be fully realized for the listener as an actual conversation. This feature of podcasts was something we had noted and discussed when listening to *All My Relations* and *The Cuts*, how the hosts or interviewer often segued to – or branched off a point made by - the other person. This emphasis on collaboration, moreover, helps to "destabilize traditional structures of power and authority and combat individualistic, capitalistic, and patriarchal values of vertical knowledge dissemination, solo discovery, and intellectual 'rigor,'" as Draucker points out ("Collaborative learning"). In other words, in a more traditional final assignment for the semester, knowledge dissemination usually takes the form of moving in one direction, from the author to the reader. In contrast, the podcast assignment ensures that knowledge dissemination moves in more than one direction. The podcast hosts share knowledge with one another, just as they collaboratively share their knowledge with the listener. And following in Draucker's footsteps here, I would argue that higher education's longstanding association between single-author work and "intellectual rigor" is specious. The podcasts that students created prove this.

The next, and final, step was the recording of the actual podcast. The Fall 2019 semester marked the first semester when the BMCC Library had available its own podcast booth. In addition to understanding the characteristics of a successful podcast, students would have to be made familiar with the podcasting equipment in the library. On the same day that the entire class visited the library to learn how to locate and evaluate secondary sources for their final assignments, the students choosing to create their own podcasts also visited the booth in pairs with a student technician, who showed them how they would be able to record and edit their podcasts when the time came for them to do so. This type of technical proficiency was a natural addition to the students' own developing familiarity with the podcast genre. Students needed to understand how to create the aural aspects of the genre, as well. As Christina M. LaVecchia explains about aural proficiency, students need to understand that aural modes are "one composing mode among many and [they have] specific capacities that sound has for creating meaning and affecting audiences" ("Materially Engaged Listening"). In other words, podcasts by nature rely on pacing and sound to make their arguments effectively, so students would need to understand how to speak and space out their argument accordingly, using the library's podcast technology.

Marty and Shawn, two students whose names I have changed for the purpose of this chapter, worked together on a podcast analyzing death and resurrection in Louise Erdrich's *Love Medicine*. Their podcast will be the focus for the remainder of this section. They not only did an exceptional job creating a podcast based on the rubric we created together, but they also showed that "intellectual rigor" can take many forms and have multiple authors, which is also why I am pleased that they agreed to share their podcast publicly on the BMCC Library's website after our semester together had ended.[1] After they introduce themselves and explain their relation to the material (as students in a Native American/Indigenous Literatures course), just as Dr. Keene and Ms.

---

[1] Due to the COVID-19 pandemic, this feature on the BMCC Library website has been delayed. I hope, however, that it is available by the time you are reading this, as the podcasts students created deserve a wide audience.

Wilbur had done, they perform a close reading of a passage about June Kashpaw, whose death essentially begins Erdrich's novel. Reading select passages from June's final living moments, Marty reads, "June had wedged herself so tight against the door that when she sprang the latch she fell out. Into the cold. It was a shock like being born... The snow fell deeper that Easter than it had in forty years, but June walked over it like water and came home" (6-7). Following this, Shawn unpacks the quotation by relating it to June's wayward lifestyle and her relationship to her family back home on the reservation. They read this passage optimistically, asserting that this moment when June leaves the car of the man she met at the bar to "c[ome] home" is evidence that she hopes to start her life in a new direction. Shawn explains, "she was tired of living her lifestyle, tired of sleeping with different guys, and she was not happy, and she get [sic] to the point where she's like, 'Okay, we will stop this.'" In fact, there are other details supporting the reading these two students provide: the fact that the cold is described as being "a shock like being born" and that June seems removed from the cold elements, described as "walk[ing] over [the snow] like water" (6, 7). Indeed, it seems, right before her untimely death, June is looking ahead to a new life for herself.

They nicely set up this close reading through a natural verbal exchange, ending when Marty says to Shawn, "I came across this quote, and I was wondering what your thoughts were on it." In this way, their podcast proves Draucker's assertion that podcasting "allow[s students] to facilitate a dynamic conversation and engage in a process of joint problem-solving and collaborative meaning-making" ("Collaborative learning"). Both students understood that they were not singularly responsible for making their argument – in fact, that they should avoid doing so due to the assignment's emphasis on collaboration. As they developed their argument, from one supporting point to the next, in each close reading they performed, they made sure to give one another space to speak and share their own interpretations. In this way, it was always clear how the students were working together to make their argument clear for the listeners. One would lead in with a quotation, and the other would provide the close reading – or vice versa.

The podcast was a way for students to realize, and practice, how to live and think "relationally," or in good relations. Marty concludes when reflecting about his partnership with Shawn, "I think we got to connect on a different level, and I think that's what this whole class is about. It's about living relationally – and with those things around you and learning to appreciate every little thing that makes up this world." Living relationally, to the students, meant deliberate reflection about the world and their roles within it. This is simply not compatible with some traditional class models that ask students to complete writing assignments before moving on to the next one. We only have fifteen weeks with students, and many times, that reality could prompt us to pack in as much content and writing assignments as possible. What the podcast assignment shows – and has taught me as an instructor – is the importance of a slow, deliberate build with the final assignment of the semester. Instead of asking students to complete a project at the end of the semester or at most a preliminary short assignment (usually a proposal) before composing the entire assignment on their own based on limited feedback, asking students to develop their projects piece by piece made the final assignment more manageable for students and instructors alike – with ample opportunity for feedback, reflection, and revision integrated into each stage of the process.

Conclusion / Possible Changes

The podcast assignment gave students the ability to connect with the course material on a more personal level. As Marty explains to us, through his partnership with Shawn, he not only got closer to a classmate but he also learned more about him, namely that the two of them were from the same island, Hispaniola: "he is Haitian, and I'm Dominican," he explains, and this source of connection no doubt increased the quality of their work. Shannon Draucker explains, "The most valuable affordance of the podcast, then, was that it made visible – or rather, audible – these webs and relations, the intellectual and affective ties among students. Through the podcast, students learned to hear and listen – and by doing so, to learn, think, and feel – *together*" ("Collaborative Learning"). In fact, prior to Marty's articulation of his and Shawn's cultural connection that they realized only while working together on the podcast, Shawn explained the "ties" he and Shawn both felt learning about Native American cultures throughout the semester. Rather than viewing the struggles and survivals of Native peoples as separate from their own, they were starting to understand the connections between the colonial histories of both the United States and the island of Hispaniola, where both students traced their cultural roots.

In addition to helping students realize their inter-cultural connections, which are often not realized in the day-to-day activities of a class that meets only twice a week, the podcast assignment fulfills some key requirements of the university's General Learning Outcomes. These outcomes were created following a 2002 revision to the Middle States standards for higher education accreditation, which "increased emphasis on outcomes assessment both for ensuring institutional effectiveness... and for the continuous improvement of teaching and learning" ("General Education Assessment Plan" 1). What this looks like from college to college, and from class to class, of course will differ. BMCC created their General Learning Outcomes from 2002-2004 through discussions with students and faculty and by linking to the practices at four-year colleges in the CUNY and SUNY systems. The BMCC General Education plan states that these efforts were meant to illuminate "what a BMCC student completing the general education requirements should know or be able to do" ("General Education Assessment Plan" 2). The phrase, "be able to do," no doubt refers to job-related skills, like critical thinking, clear writing, and public speaking, among others, but in addition to these, the specific skills I decided to emphasize in this class, and that the podcast assignment helped prioritize, were related to metacognition, multicultural awareness, empathy, and connection: understanding what brings us together and what we can do to improve our relations.

While the sequence of assignments leading up to the podcast helped me stress these skills, there are certainly some practices I would consider going forward. The auditory nature of podcasts, for instance, requires that students speak clearly enough to be understood: this, however, could discourage students with accents or who feel that their own grasp on English is too tenuous from attempting to create their podcast. While I have no definitive answer on how best to address this, one suggestion I received[2] that could be of particular benefit would be to encourage ESL students to speak in their own language, translating into English whenever it is necessary. This practice could function as a link to the ongoing language revitalization efforts that we discussed in class throughout the semester in many Native/Indigenous communities. Just as we open our classroom space to a variety of Native languages, students can expand our linguistic scope even further by using their own cultural language. Additionally, I would like to have a post-semester discussion with the students who created podcasts to solicit any suggestions they have about changing the rubric: are there any skills that they feel they developed that the rubric does not sufficiently account for?

Ultimately, the podcast assignment breaks the monotony, for students and instructors alike, of the research essay assignment, which Composition Studies scholars like Kerry Dirk point out are viewed by students as having only limited relevance to their overall education ("The 'Research Paper' Prompt"). Podcasts disrupt our ongoing emphasis on singularly created and developed work – as if any worthwhile work we do is completed in isolation. Even this single-author essay, for instance, has benefitted from the feedback and suggestions of others. Podcasts also bring to light the backgrounds and interests that bring us together, to the classroom space, instead of what separates us, like the endless pursuit for high grades or the ideal internship or job. In this way, then, the

---

[2] I presented an earlier version of this paper at the annual Northeast Modern Language Association (NeMLA) conference in Boston, MA, in 2021. Many thanks to the audience members who provided insightful suggestions.

podcast assignment becomes one way in which we can truly decolonize the classroom, interrogating how the histories of colonialism impact our classroom experiences together and rightfully disrupting them.

Bibliography

Bazerman, Charles. "Writing Speaks to Situations Through Recognizable Forms." *Naming What We Know: Threshold Concepts of Writing Studies*, edited by Linda Adler-Kassner and Elizabeth Wardle. University Press of Colorado, 2015, pp. 35-37.

Cole, Rick and Beth Kramer. "Podcasts and the Twenty-First Century College Classroom." *BU Center for Interdisciplinary Teaching & Learning*, http://sites.bu.edu/impact/previous-issues/impact-summer-2017/podcasts-and-the-twenty-first-century-college-classroom/. Accessed 31 Oct. 2020.

Dirk, Kerry. "The 'Research Paper' Prompt: A Dialogic Opportunity for Transfer." *Composition Forum*, vol. 25, http://compositionforum.com/issue/25/research-paper-prompt-transfer.php. Accessed 31 Dec. 2020.

Draucker, Shannon. "Audible Networks: Podcasts and Collaborate Learning. Hybrid Pedagogy, 16 July 2020, https://hybridpedagogy.org/audible-networks-podcasts-and-collaborative-learning/. Accessed 27 Dec. 2020.

Driscoll, Dana Lynn. "Connected, Disconnected, or Uncertain: Student Attitudes about Future Writing Contexts and Perceptions of Transfer from First Year Writing to the Disciplines."*Across the Disciplines*, vol. 8, no. 2, 2011, https://wac.colostate.edu/docs/atd/articles/driscoll2011.pdf. Accessed 31 Dec. 2020.

Estrem, Heidi. "Writing Is A Knowledge-Making Activity." *Naming What We Know: Threshold Concepts of Writing Studies*, edited by Linda Adler-Kassner and Elizabeth Wardle. University Press of Colorado, 2015, pp. 19-20.

"General Education Assessment Plan." BMCC Assessment, https://www.bmcc.cuny.edu/wp-content/uploads/ported/iresearch/upload/GenEdplan.pdf. Accessed 29 Dec. 2020.

Glaser, Hollis. "What makes a meaningful assignment?" *CUNY Academic Commons*, 23 Nov. 2018, https://glaser100.commons.gc.cuny.edu/2018/11/23/what-makes-a-meaningful-assignment/. Accessed 26 Dec. 2020.

Harjo, Sterlin, host. "Louise Erdrich." *The Cuts*, 3 Jan. 2017, https://www.indianandcowboy.com/episodes/2017/1/3/the-cuts-episode-14-louise-erdrich. Accessed on 31 Dec. 2020.

Keene, Adrienne and Matika Wilbur, hosts. "All My Relations and Indigenous Feminism." *All My Relations*, 26 Feb. 2019, https://www.allmyrelationspodcast.com/podcast/episode/32b0bd95/ep-1-all-my-relations-and-indigenous-feminism. Accessed on 28 Dec. 2020.

LaVecchia, Christina M. "Toward a Pedagogy of Materially Engaged Listening." *Composition Forum*, vol. 35, Spring 2017, http://compositionforum.com/issue/35/listening.php. Accessed 31 Dec. 2020.

Mammina, Alix. "Teaching the Art of Listening: How to Use Podcasts in the Classroom. *Education Week*, 14 Sept. 2017, https://blogs.edweek.org/teachers/

teaching_now/2017/09/teaching_the_art_of_listening_how_to_use_podcasts_in_the_classroom.html. Accessed 31 Oct. 2020.

Rivero, Victor. "What is Unlearning." *EdTechDigest*, 13 July 2017, https://edtechdigest.com/2017/07/13/what-is-unlearning/. Accessed on 14 May 2020.

Tinberg, Howard. "Metacognition Is Not Cognition." *Naming What We Know: Threshold Concepts of Writing Studies*, edited by Linda Adler-Kassner and Elizabeth Wardle. University Press of Colorado, 2015, pp. 75-76.

Wiley, David. "What Is Open Pedagogy?" Open Content, 21 Oct. 2013, https://opencontent.org/blog/archives/2975. Accessed on 24 Dec. 2020.

Chapter 2

Adding to Archives, Stories, and Conversations: Dramaturgy, Collaboration, and the Non-terminating Essay Assignment

Aoise Stratford
Cornell University

Abstract

The concept of student work that contributes to public knowledge is at the center of Aoise Stratford's (Cornell University) "Adding to Archives, Stories, and Conversations," in which she offers a number of strategies for fostering scholarly collaboration, reframing the end-of-term essay as an entry rather than an endpoint. In one assignment, for example, students conduct research to propose a text to be used in the course the next time it's offered; another assignment asks students to find intersections with other classes, adding to an archive that outlives the individual syllabus; and a third assignment functions as a kind of collaboratively built literature review that future students can draw on, and then, in turn, contribute to. This chapter includes both sample assignment prompts with accompanying rationales and grading strategies for both analytical and creative work, as well as application to both in-person and online teaching situations.

Keywords: Diversity, Equity, and Inclusion (DEI), nontraditional writing assignments, writing about dramatic literature, collaborative assignments

***

Introduction: Why This, Here, Now?

Both in my own practice as a playwright and dramaturg, and also in the classroom when I am teaching those disciplines, I find myself always returning to collaboration. How do we connect to each other? What questions do we need to ask in order to foster important conversations among artists, audiences, writers, actors, readers, and critics? How might compassionate and imaginative leaps of faith help us generate narratives and embodied experiences that can reach across boundaries to our shared humanity? In a sense, all of these questions have at their heart the question of how the work we do as individuals benefits others, contributing to a shared vision of the world and its many complexities and contradictions. This paper is not about teaching dramaturgy, per se, but it is about how a dramaturgical sensibility—a finely-tuned phronetic approach to supporting, fostering and improving the work of collaborators engaged in making something together for an audience[1]—might open opportunities to reimagine the end-of-term student essay. In such reimaginings, we can engage students in work that functions not as an ending or a final word, but rather as the beginning of new connections and conversations, and as a new contribution to a shared, ongoing, and ever-evolving archive of thinking and writing.

A key question that dramaturgs routinely confront is "why this, why here, why now?" (Chemers 108, Lang 79) and this essay must begin with this same question. Why indeed? Why this particular approach to designing and implementing the work we ask students to make? Why here in a liberal arts college? Why in this moment? For one thing, the global health crisis prompted by COVID-19 has, in 2020, both driven student learning and classroom communities online and made urgent the need to reconsider course structures. Challenging as it has been, this moment has also generated unique opportunities to reshape assignments, syllabi and lesson plans, and to be more dynamic in the ways in which we think about classroom communities, and, within those communities, the ways in which we approach asynchronous work and online platforms for both learning and storing knowledge. This moment also offers us the chance to forge new communities of students that extend beyond the classroom, beyond the local community, existing nationally and internationally. The non-terminating assignment has greater relevance for this expanded model of the classroom because it seeks to free up the exchange of ideas between students. Rather than suggesting that learning happens from a teacher to a homogenous group, the renewable or non-terminating assignment encourages student-to-student learning. In this moment, when connection between students is key to combatting the pandemic's virtual isolation, and when students from a wider variety of backgrounds, socio-political, cultural

---

[1] Dramaturgy is notoriously hard to define because the work of a dramaturg is rooted in collaboration, highly variable, and often difficult to point to in the end product of theatre. In his introduction to *Ghost Light*, Michael Chemers draws on Aristotle's notion of *Phronesis* as a kind of "practical wisdom…employed to advance the greater good" (Chemers, 5).

and geographical locations might come together, such assignments have clear utility.

The non-terminating assignments proposed here are cumulative as well as communal in their approach. By shaping our assignments such that all students can think across courses, and across generations of the same course, we invite our students to make meaningful connections between each other, between what they study and do in other courses, and what others study and do, also. To some extent this is at the foundation of the liberal arts education, which values intellectual breadth and connectivity, diversity and inclusivity, as skills for social and civic engagement—and as skills for life. And indeed, despite widespread anxiety about the health of liberal arts colleges in this moment of high tech, budget cuts, and corporatization, as Matthew Moen recently argued, the liberal arts emphasis on inclusive thinking and good citizenry is more urgent now than ever ("Opportunity Knocks").[2]

A further effect of emphasizing student work as cumulative rather than terminating is that non-terminating assignments inherently challenge canon formation. With a call for institutions across America to question assumptions about what gets taught and how we might collectively diversify and "decolonize that syllabus" (Dechavez), an assignment that positions students' work as writing of value to other students clearly helps foster a more inclusive approach. This is not to devalue canonical texts but rather to value students' work as part of an ongoing history, one in which they can actively participate. My thinking here again borrows from theatre practice, encouraging students to work with the principle of the classic acting and improvisation exercise: "*Yes, and...,*" which requires us to accept, collaborate, and contribute, rather than reject ("Yes, And!").

The first assignment discussed is a research-based, 'add to the archive' paper that allows students to propose a text for the course next time around. This assignment is structured to include both comparative analysis and argument, thus building traditional and valuable writing skills while also framing student thinking and writing as something with value for future students. The second assignment asks students to respond creatively to a text already on the syllabus and requires an analytical rationale that supports their own creative work. This assignment meets different kinds of learners with different skill sets, experiences, and interests where they are and is structured to help students find intersections with other classes and/or generate projects that outlive the class in other ways.

---

[2] Moen's primary concern in this piece is the value afforded critical inquiry and truth seeking in a liberal education, qualities that he identifies as both essential to the future of democracy and rooted in the kind of broad inclusivity and transparency that I am proposing this dramaturgical approach seeks to foster.

By emphasizing creative engagement with a text, this assignment seeks to underscore the relationship between creativity and critical analysis as a relationship that is mutually informative, generative, and potentially circular rather than necessarily linear and finite. The third assignment addressed here asks students to contribute to a blog that collaboratively builds a list of shared resources. This particular assignment helps students develop a specific set of dramaturgical, writing and analytical skills that situate what the students consume in a larger context and can function as a kind of collaboratively built literature review, a glossary, or an encyclopedic archive. All these assignments offer a bridge between the conventional but disposable argument or analysis paper and a piece of writing that accomplishes those same ends but does so in a way that both allows students to exercise choice and agency, and also ensures ongoing pedagogical value.

Adding To The Archive Research Assignment

The Adding to the Archive assignment is, in essence, a simple argument paper reframed to keep pedagogical implications open. I have taught this assignment in several courses and its simplicity makes it highly adaptable to a wide variety of literature review, genre, or historical survey courses. One course I teach looks at vampire narratives across a range of media and cultural contexts to consider the ways in which social anxieties about race, sexuality and gender are articulated by one of our most pervasive myths. In that course, the Add to the Archive paper serves as the last formal paper students write for the class, though it is taken up in several ways after it is turned in, a point to which I will return in a moment. The initial prompt looks something like this:

> Write a paper in which you argue for the inclusion of a particular text in the syllabus for this course. You can write on anything—as long as it either features a vampire in a prominent role in the narrative or you can make a strong case for the piece's meaning as being articulated specifically through the tonal or metaphorical register of vampire iconography and lore. Don't just pick your favorite vampire movie or video game, interrogate your choice. Explain why this text is different, exemplary, ground-breaking, productively problematic, culturally significant, fills a useful gap, etc—not just why it is 'good.'

One of the benefits of this paper is student buy-in. Because it allows them to choose broadly, they are able to write about a text that holds deep interest, and yet because the prompt for the paper is specific (argue for inclusion), it encourages focused engagement with course content. This combination of wide choice with limited structural parameters has, in my classes at least, tended to generate successful papers. Students work on a number of writing skills to generate this paper, including summary (introducing their chosen text), synthesis (integration of sources from class and outside class), comparative and contextual analysis (situating the text in terms of course materials, genres, cultural movements, etc.), and argument development (appropriate concession, tone, and logical progression). In these ways, the paper aims to accomplish many of the learning outcomes that end of term essays might normally demand in terms of research, critical thinking, and writing skills.

An obvious downside of the invitation for students to exercise agency and cast the net widely is that the instructor may find themselves unfamiliar with the topic of a student's paper, generating a need for investing time in order to become familiar—at least familiar enough to be in meaningful conversation about the paper. However, this happens less often than one might think and, when it does happen, there may be a benefit in gaining familiarity with new material. Particularly in the realm of contemporary media, I recognize that I can't possibly know everything that is out there. Foregoing the need to be an expert in a top-down class model affords me the opportunity to empower my students to be agents of their own learning and to think of themselves as valued contributors to a conversation where all voices might be heard and all experiences are of equal value.

Student work is informed by the course as the paper calls for them to situate their suggested addition to the archive in the context of the primary and secondary resources already on the syllabus, but student work also informs the course, making possible rich discussions about selection and canonization. In an ideal semester, I assign this near the end of term with enough time to have class discussion about everyone's proposed text. In-class exercises can include a short two-minute pitch from students as a verbal/visual presentation that highlights their choice. Having students then vote on their top two choices can also lead to robust discussion about selection and how syllabi are shaped. I have found these conversations to be very powerful indeed. I am surprised that often students have not thought that much about the way courses are curated. I have consequently found it very productive to be transparent about my own selection of material, drawing attention to gaps, opportunities, potential overlaps or new directions in these discussions. This, I believe, helps my students become more discerning consumers of media.

One thing the pedagogical practice of working with this assignment has opened up in my teaching is the possibility of leaving open spaces for student-supplied content in my syllabi. I am currently experimenting with having students 'add to the archive' not as a reflection that frames their work-so-far and offers value for future students, but rather having them add to the archive (or rather, the syllabus) from the beginning. In this context the greatest value is for the community of learners to which they are the most directly connected –

their fellow students and instructor in the class – but the texts they bring in to work with may become part of the syllabus as it is reinvented the next semester, and the one after that, and so on. At the time of this writing, I am putting together a syllabus for a survey class on contemporary drama by women. There are obviously far more wonderful and worthy plays by women than can possibly be taught in a single semester or indeed a lifetime, so why not choose, say six, and leave the other two slots open? In this version of the assignment, the students will be tasked with adding to the archive and decolonizing the syllabus by proposing one to three titles or writers they're curious to learn more about. In our second or third week of classes, students will share their recommendations and offer a brief presentation or pitch that explains why they chose them (analysis! argument!) and then we'll decide as a group. While I confess to some trepidation about the logistics of this exercise (and the labor it may generate in shaping the class), I'm excited by the possibilities that refashioning this ending as a beginning might generate for engaging students in critical thinking and discussion about the power of choice, canonization, selection, bias and pedagogy.

Adding to The Story Creative Assignment

The second assignment discussed here engages a text already on a course syllabus and requires the students to use focused close reading, analysis of that text and critical thinking as the launch pad for creative expression. One of the great benefits of this assignment is the ways in which it meets different kinds of learners with different skill sets, experiences, and interests where they are, and allows them to approach course content and discursive expectations, which may be challenging, unfamiliar – or even too familiar – from a different angle rooted in their own voices or interests. As James Lang notes in a recent piece on distraction in the classroom, creativity helps break through the "attention-dulling routines that affect our classrooms" ("Distracted Minds"). I have taught versions of this "add to the story" assignment in several historical/genre survey classes and in first year academic writing seminars. It is typically one of the most popular assignments I teach and tends to generate extremely rich, thoughtful and exciting work.

Two somewhat different versions of this assignment require elaboration here in order to show how they serve learning goals, how they generate student investment with implications that extend beyond the current classroom context, and how they might be implemented in a variety of courses.

The first example comes from a first-year academic writing seminar, which, as I teach it in its current version, is organized around detective narratives and calls for students to write a number of essays as they develop college level writing skills. This assignment specifically values creativity in a class that is not necessarily "creative" in its focus and does not necessarily draw a student population who think of themselves as creative writers. By bringing creativity into the traditionally non-creative classroom, this assignment sets up a relationship between a student's individual creative expression and the practices of academic reading and writing that situates them as mutually informative and equally valuable.

The assignment begins, as many do, with reading. One text I have found particularly successful for this academic writing assignment is Elinor Fuchs's widely popular and wonderful dramaturgical essay, "Visit To A Small Planet." This essay nicely exemplifies Lang's argument that "the poet's…creative turns of language" can help students to refocus their attention and look more closely at what they might otherwise miss ("Distracted Minds"). Full of provocative questions, poetic images and sustained metaphor, Fuchs encourages readers to look at a story as if it were a whole alien world, rich in small unique detail and meaningful patterns. As I have written elsewhere, I have (in this class at least) typically paired Fuchs's short essay with Susan Glaspell's short play *Trifles*,[3] but Fuchs is widely applicable and the assignment is infinitely adaptable. For example, in this same class I often also pair this reading with one of several short stories, which, while not drama, are nonetheless small, detailed worlds, well-served by Fuchs's guide for close reading. Fuchs makes clear the importance of considering both what is present in a text and what is not, and she frames this consideration in terms that are useful to the academic writing classroom:

> Make sure you're alert to what's there; there should be actual *evidence* on the planet for what you *report*….In most dramatic worlds there are [also] hidden, or at least unseen, spaces. Ask *questions* about them as well….How do they *relate* to the *represented* world, the world you can see? (Fuchs 7, emphasis added)

In this particular example, Glaspell's play *Trifles* offers a rich tapestry of visible evidence. Glaspell is specific in her detail of the character's movements as they "look fearfully about" and "stand close together," and of the play's setting, "a gloomy kitchen, and left without having been put in order…unwashed pans in the sink," etc. (Glaspell 26). This setting is the space for the investigation of the murder of John Wright, a farmer, by (presumably) his wife, Minnie. Yet though they are the topic of the other characters' conversation and the original inhabitants of the play's atmospheric environment, neither John nor Minnie

---

[3] My forthcoming chapter, "Teaching Trifles in The Writing Room" (Gainor, J. E. (ed), *Susan Glaspell in Context*, CUP), provides details about this assignment but focuses primarily on versions of it with specific utility for introductory playwriting classes.

ever appears on stage. This mix of detail and absence provides students with much evidence to analyze, and much room for creative speculation. Importantly, while *Trifles* is ideal for this assignment on a class that coheres around detective narratives, any text that gestures to a world and people beyond its immediate set and action (and a great many do) can serve equally well.

Having read both Fuchs and *Trifles*, students are asked to focus on the absent characters. An in-class worksheet guides students in small collaborative groups through preparatory work thusly:

> Make a list of at least five things people say (either directly or by implication) about Minnie. Note who says what and whether you agree (and if you don't, why not!). Then write a brief description of Minnie that tells us about her personality/psychology, her physicality, and the social forces that inform her character. Choose precise adjectives and specific details. Do the same for John.

Playwright and dramaturg Will Dunne's helpful definition of character as a "complex blend of physical, psychological, and social traits" (Dunne 3) provides a useful framework for students to focus on the task of noting observations that can be used as support for brief character descriptions. Students then use this preparatory work as the basis for writing their own creative scene between Minnie and John. The first part of the prompt goes like this:

> <u>Part One</u>: Write a brief scene (1-2 pages) that shows us a moment that is important but *not* shown in the existing story. Think carefully about how the characters you are writing about behave. How do you know what they would do or say? Draw on the preparatory work we have done gathering evidence and analyzing characters to help you invent with specific detail. Remember, analysis aims to answer the question "how does it work?" so let your scene demonstrate your understanding of how the characters (and the story world they inhabit) work.

One challenge of offering creative assignments in academic writing courses stems from how to approach grading such assignments in line with existing class rubrics, and how the assignment engages learning goals focused on things like mechanics, thesis development and analytical reading. Both concerns are easily addressed by the inclusion of a rationale. Hence, this assignment requires that the creative scene be accompanied by a rationale in which students must analyze and cite Glaspell's text to support their own creative choices about how Minnie and John behave and speak in the creative scene. This second part of the prompt looks like this:

Part Two: Write a brief rationale (about 2 pages) that provides an analysis of the scene you wrote. Your job here is to provide a written explanation for why the characters you chose to write about behave the way they do in the scene you have written – or put another way how your scene reveals those characters to us. In this rationale you will be making claims about those characters and using the original text to support those claims.

The labor of writing an analytical rationale for their own creative literary work takes the exercise well past the bounds of mimicry to consciously re-emphasize the mutually informed and circular relationship between writing and reading, between creativity and analysis. As such, this assignment both values creativity as expression but also as a means to perform what dramaturg Lenora Inez Brown emphasizes as "active listening," a kind of listening that is rooted in asking open questions, imagining possibilities, and paying attention to what is not on the page, as well as what is there. This kind of listening is mindful of context and, Brown argues, promotes "strong understanding" and "clarifies communication" (xvii).

Further, the rationale itself provides the instructor with a piece of writing more specifically demonstrative of the elements of traditional academic writing. As such, I have found the rationale a helpful tool in assessing the following stated learning goals for this particular class:

- Students will learn and be able to demonstrate skills for reading closely, carefully, and analytically, and responding thoughtfully to assigned course content.
- Students will learn and be able to demonstrate effective and coherent organization of an essay's claims and evidence.
- Students will develop an awareness of their processes, practice, and voices as writers.
- Students will learn to identify, and create, writing that is clear and demonstrates appropriate use of grammar, punctuation, word-choice, and diction.

In this way, regardless of what kind of grading system or contract is in place, the rationale provides a way to assess how students are meeting specific class goals while the scene itself, which I grade on completion and effort, not on "talent," engages the students in the course's content. Grading the assignment this way takes the pressure off students to second-guess what might be "good" story writing and to focus instead on exploring their own creative voices. Such an approach values students' voices equally and, in keeping with the tenets of contract grading, "allows students the freedom to take risks, and try new things in their writing" (Inoue 142). Inoue's approach to labor-based grading serves as a means to dismantle white writing privilege, valuing effort over quality (Inoue 138-139), and in classes where more traditional grading structures are used, separating this assignment into two parts—one graded on completion, one measured against articulated learning goals—supports diversity, encourages exploration, and provides some rewarding flexibility for both instructors and students.

A second version of this assignment also bears some further mention here. This is a version I have adapted for, and taught in, theatre and media survey classes where the focus is not on academic writing but on understanding key course content: critical methodologies, histories, movements, texts, etc. While these classes are not craft-based practical theatre classes so much as historical or critical classes, they nonetheless tend to have a student population that is variously interested in theatre and media from a practical standpoint. Consequently, the "add to the story" assignment here can take a variety of forms. One implementation I have found particularly durable and flexible is to require students to complete one creative assignment (with supporting rationale) but to give them three options, spaced throughout the semester, from which to choose. Many times, students select to do this assignment at the end of the term as a way to bring what they have learned practically to bear on other skills and ongoing interests, but regardless of where in the semester it falls, the work serves to benefit the other learners in the class, too.

Options all center on texts covered during the semester and may include the making of short performances, short films or trailers, written scripts for scenes not already present (as per the earlier example), presentations on lighting, set or costume designs, program notes, posters, bills or flyers, and reviews for theoretical productions. The variety of options here is designed to allow students to choose something that they are very invested in or passionate about trying, and/or something that allows them to work in ways that accommodate their individual strengths, voices, and working methods. Some students are very visual thinkers, for example, and an assignment that allows them to approach course content in a way that allows for the visual and spatial has obvious advantages.

In each case, the accompanying rationale offers students the space to write about their creative choices in a way that explains both their own creative process and thinking, and also their understanding of the assigned texts, content, and context. For example, critical questions explored might include:

- o How does this review speak to the technical innovations on the early nineteenth century London stage and the ways in which audiences would have experienced Gothic melodrama?

- How does this performance embody the notion of ritual as it applies to early dance drama? How does it take up understandings of space and spectator?
- How does this portfolio of costume sketches inform us about the gender politics and social concerns at work in Ibsen's play?

This assignment is highly flexible and easily adapted to different courses and classrooms – including the online classroom. The responses I have had to this assignment have been rich and varied, with students generating scripts, posters, music, performances, choreography, reviews, sketches, lighting plots, soundscapes, collages, cartoons, and more.

Clearly, the down-side is that the instructor might often find themselves outside their area of expertise. I am no musician, that's for sure! However, the rationale and presentation are specifically engineered to be tools for highlighting the creative work's exploration and evocation of an assigned text (or genre, etc.) in terms of its conventions, innovations, features, themes, politics, reception, and aesthetics. And again, that verbal and written work is assessable in terms of a student's research, writing, and demonstrated understanding of course materials. Furthermore, there are several advantages of this assignment that speak specifically to its collaborative and non-terminating qualities.

Firstly, the assignment is structured to help students find intersections with other classes. If a student is also taking costume design, for example, or a class in visual art, cartooning, or architectural design, it provides avenues to continue "learning by doing," as students gain extra practice working with that discipline. Hence an assignment like this can be mutually supportive of what students are learning in other classes, giving it utility and purpose beyond a single class. So too, projects started as creative assignments in a critically or historically focused class may very well outlive the class in other ways, finding their way into other classes, clubs, or community events, adding to an ongoing archive of student work with relevance beyond the syllabus. Secondly, creative skills are transferable skills and a pedagogy that accommodates creativity helps to foster awareness of the relationship between the making of art and literature and the use or study of art and literature.

Lastly, when students present their creative work, they introduce others to their discipline, areas of experience, and interests. Current trends towards peer teaching de-center the instructor as the sole authority and open spaces for students to function not as consumers but "as producers" of class content, who learn by teaching and thus "can act as really powerful agents and collaborators towards their own understanding and that of their peers as well," as Simon Bates of The University of British Columbia's Center for Teaching, Learning and

Technology found in one such pedagogical project ("From Consumer to Creator"). The task of articulating their ideas as they share their presentation is a helpful tool for students as they draft the rationale, allowing them to gain valuable feedback about how to impart knowledge or experience that is not necessarily shared by their peers. This is, of course, a valuable skill on the job market and beyond, but significantly for course structure it offers a valuable opportunity to learn from each other, disrupting the traditional hierarchical instruction mode that has tended to dominate end-of-term work and assessment.

Adding To The Conversation Collaborative Assignment

The last of the three assignment models addressed here is more collaborative in design. With the widespread move to online learning platforms, some opportunities for student collaborations have been made more difficult. Certainly break-out rooms can bring dispersed students together in smaller online collaborative groups for discussion or work on focused tasks, but classroom environments like labs, studios and rehearsal rooms, in which students *make* things together, have had to be rethought. So too, discussion boards can sometimes result in traffic that mimics transitory chat rather than functions as scaffolding for something with lasting and significant impact for all the students in the class. The goal of this assignment is to have students collaborate on the writing of a document that is bigger than the sum of its collective parts and that is intended for further use in that it can be read, discussed, added to, revised, or used as a resource in future classes.

The inspiration for this assignment once again has roots in a dramaturgical pedagogy. As Lang explains, the dramaturg's "casebook" is "a document created in order to capture...contextual materials" providing a "useful repository of valuable information" for a collaborative community (T. Lang 115-116). Casebooks used in rehearsal for theatre productions often include things such as biographical information, research on genre or period, theory and criticism helpful to reading the play, maps, timelines, images, a glossary of references that appear in the script, information relevant to the socio-political context of the play, character bios, previous production history (in some cases including critical reception), guides to pronunciation or translation or the meaning of unfamiliar terms, and any other information determined by context that is pertinent to the collaborative work of the team (T. Lang 115, Chemers 148, 152).

In my most recent dramaturgy class I asked my students to collaboratively select a play that we could produce a casebook for. They chose Sarah Ruhl's *Orlando*, a wonderful contemporary adaptation of Virginia Woolf's novel by the same name, which perhaps not so coincidentally for my pedagogical purpose here defers finality, and embraces flexibility, openness, and curiosity in order to underscore "the illusory nature of endings" (Ruhl xiii). Students then independently decided on a piece to contribute to the casebook. One student provided a comparative biography of Woolf and Ruhl, another traced references to a particular poem, another provided an annotated timeline of the play, others provided glossary entries that shared information about the play's locations, people, objects, and references, others provided footnotes to particular themes or details that occur in the novel but not in the adaptation, and so on and so on. This assignment required that students

> ...work collaboratively to select a play for which we will create a casebook made up of individual entries. Having chosen a play for a hypothetical production as a class, each student will then generate one written entry that demonstrates their own research, citation and writing. Each entry will focus on an aspect of the play that can be illuminated by the provision of context. Entries should be clear and economical and written consciously with the reader (user) in mind. They should be expositional and analytical, not argumentative. Why did you choose this aspect of the play as a significant one for enhancing our reading of the original text (not just satisfying a minor curiosity)? Consider who you imagine will use your document: What might a director find beneficial? Or a designer, or actor? How does the context you provide help us understand why this play, now, for this theatre and its audience?

While this assignment has very specific application here, it has clear utility for liberal arts classes focused on theory and history, as well as those engaged more directly in practice. In this sense, the dramaturg's casebook can be adapted to function as a kind of collaboratively built study guide. Such documents, and the entries that make them up, might find their final form in class blogs or websites, databases, educational packets for schools, or even in open access resources such as library archives, Wikipedia or doolee. Further, while in its above form it was taught mid-semester for reasons that had to do with the institutional calendar and guest speakers, this sort of work is ideal for an end of semester project that serves as a collaborative capstone with genuine value beyond the classroom.

In the simplest terms, the dramaturg's casebook assignment asks students to collaboratively build a shared document. Yet it does not have to be as complex or as individually tailored as the previous example suggests. The document may, for example, comprise similar entries on a range of texts, rather than a range of entries on one shared primary source. In this context the collaboratively built document may be a blog for a collection of reviews or recommendations, much as one might find a list of "staff pick" recommendations in an independent bookstore, or it may be an annotated bibliography for course materials (or supplemental course materials) that can be put into service in future classes, or (more in keeping with the original notebook assignment) a series of footnotes to a course text or texts. It may take the form of a glossary of terms that offers definitions for key words and concepts pertinent to the course's subject matter or methodologies, or to particular units within it, or it may take the form of any collaboratively brainstormed list that might benefit from written elaboration and serve as a communicative tool for another audience of learners or collaborators. It is enormously flexible.

One obvious application of this assignment functions as a more economical version of the Add to the Archive assignment. In such a version, students post pitches for objects of study they think engage class subject matter and that deserve the attention of their peers – the community that ultimately functions as the readers and end-users in this scenario. In this version of the assignment students have to write economically while still putting forward a well-supported argument. As with the longer version of this assignment, they have to argue for how the text they are pitching makes an important contribution to our semester-long course conversation – not just why they like it. Hence this version gives student writers useful practice in concision, adhering to the dramaturgical principle that documents produced for collaboration "must be useful" and "held to the bar of efficacy" in order to be constructive for the user for which it is purposefully intended (T. Lang 32).

In my detective narrative class one particularly rewarding end-of-term exercise had students read everyone's posts and then discuss them as a class. A more engaging variation on the "okay-what-did-we-learn" wrap up discussion, the focus of this discussion was to decide which pitch best exemplified the themes, conventions and politics of the other texts we had looked at over the course of the semester, giving us a chance to meaningfully reflect on the critical questions the course sought to address, and bring those questions to bear on the television shows, movies, and books the students were drawn to outside of class. The winning text (an episode of *How To Get Away With Murder*) was added to the syllabus the following time the class was taught. Students were excited about the idea of paying it forward, and the conversations we had about canon formation, popular media, and course design empowered students to think more deeply about the media they get exposed to and consume.

End-of-term assignments that invite students to work together to make something, to "add to the story," have the power to help build community – both among the students in the class this semester, and those that might follow them. And further, by inviting students to both reflect consciously on the reader for whom they write and also to share their own reading experiences, such assignments pedagogically underscore the importance of situating what we read, watch, see, play, and listen to in larger discursive contexts.

Conclusion

The assignments discussed here emphasize reading, thinking and writing skills that meet learning goals for students: research, citation, claim, support, tone, concision, audience, and analysis. However, and perhaps even more vitally, they are also structured to foster scholarly collaboration and contribution. In doing so, the hope is that by adding to archives, stories and conversations, terminating essays and assignments can be reframed as points of entry into larger and ongoing creative and academic conversations. That Wiley's call for non-disposable assignments found immediate synergy with my own teaching philosophy, and with the teaching of many of my colleagues,[4] suggests these larger conversations will continue to grow. While the intention is to meet individual students where they are, spark their own specific interests, and stimulate individual student agency over the learning process, what may indeed be most valuable here is that these assignments offer ongoing pedagogical value for all the learners in the class (including the instructor), not just for the student in question.

Bibliography

Brown, Lenora Inez. *New Play Development*. Focus / Hackett Publishing, 2015.

Chemers, Michael. *Ghost Light: An Introductory Handbook for Dramaturgy*. Southern Illinois University Press, 2010.

DeChavez, Yvette. "It's Time To Decolonize That Syllabus." *The Los Angeles Times*, 8 October 2018.

Dunne, Will *The Dramatic Writer's Companion*. Second Edition. Chicago: University of Chicago Press, 2009, 2017.

"From Consumer to Creator: Students as Producers of Content." *University of British Columbia Flexible Learning*, 18 Feb. 2015, http://flexible.learning.ubc.ca/case-studies/simon-bates/.

Fuchs, Elinor. "Visit To A Small Planet: Some Questions to Ask a Play." *Theater*, Volume 34, Number 2, Summer 2004, pp. 4-9.

Glaspell, Susan. "Trifles." S*usan Glaspell The Complete Plays*. Jefferson: McFarland & Co., 2010, pp. 26-34.

Inoue, Asao B. *Labor-Based Grading Contracts: Building Equity and Inclusion in the Compassionate Writing Classroom*. CSU Press, 2019.

Lang, James. "Distracted Minds: Why You Should Teach Like A Poet." *The Chronicle of Higher Education*, www.chronicle.com, 4 December 2020.

Lang, Teresa. *Essential Dramaturgy: The Mindset and Skillset*. Routledge, 2017

---

[4] Several of my colleagues are teaching with similar ideas and have been a wonderful and collegial source of inspiration for my own teaching here at Cornell: Nick Salvato has an add to archive assignment, Juan Munoz has had students work with wikipedia, Tao Goffe works with footnotes and Jenny Mann uses blogs—there are doubtless many more examples!

Moen, Matthew. "Opportunity Knocks for Liberal Education" *Inside Higher Ed*, www.insidehighered.com, 17 December 2020.

Ruhl, Sarah. *Chekov's Three Sisters and Woolf's Orlando: Two Renderings For The Stage*. Theatre Communications Group, 2013.

"Yes, And! Drama Game." *Drama Notebook,* dramanotebook.com/drama-games/yes-and/. Accessed 9 January 2021.

Chapter 3

Comparative Reading by Students in the World: For Promoting Better Understanding of Literature and Peace in the World

Akiyoshi Suzuki

Nagasaki University, Japan

Abstract

Akiyoshi Suzuki (Nagasaki University) is also interested in crossing cultural boundaries in "Comparative Reading by Students in the World." Suzuki challenges the East-West cultural divide with an international student collaboration that can enrich and augment the work of comparative literature researchers. By contributing to this online resource, students see that their own observations and insights have value outside their own classroom, as they discover unexpected affinities between literary texts of different cultures.

Keywords: East-West Comparative Literature, collaborative assignments, pedagogy

***

Introduction

In our globalized society, persons of letters would promote, I hope, not ethnocentrism but respect for diversity. However, as the distinguished scholar of American literature Walter Benn Michaels has highlighted in *The Shape of the Signifier* and *The Trouble with Diversity*, imagining a world of differences without disagreements and their overly enthusiastic defense could further peoples' fragmentation and indifference to the (putative) Other. In such a world, people could live without addressing the problem of the subject articulated through its relation to an oppressive norm, by respecting (or ignoring) all differences or by referring to postmodern theory "commit[ted] to making true and false interpretations impossible and thus to eliminating interpretation itself" (*Shape of the Signifier* 80). Paradoxically, one basic, significant global affinity is that human societies strictly prohibit denial of one another. Thus, people live by staging parallel marches, as if to say, "This is your story and this is my story, but they do not affect each other" so that "the very idea of an interpretive dispute disappears" (*Shape of the Signifier* 116). Such parallel marches preclude mutual understanding and promote social and global human fragmentation and indifference, ending in ethnocentrism. Michaels regards such a phenomenon as "the project of the end of history," as in Francis Fukuyama's view of society after the collapse of the Berlin Wall or in a globalized society. Of course, Michaels rejects the project, thus tacitly advocating that civilizations again argue their differences.

Here however, I ask the fundamental question, "Do people's imaginations, speculations, conceptions, cognitions, and expressions predominantly differ?" Zhang Longxi, distinguished scholar of comparative studies upon whose ideas I rely in this chapter's argument, persuasively suggests that although many scholars focus on fundamental differences and even emphasize incommensurability with reference to Thomas Kuhn and some postmodern theorists, differences can be found through comparison, which is possible from the perspective of affinity among candidates. Indeed, tallying differences indicates—whether consciously or unconsciously—*awareness of affinity*. In fact, there are no affinities without differences and no differences without affinities. As Zhang argues, "Difference and affinity—the specific and the general, the diverse and the universal—are all complementary to one another with emphasis put on one side or the other; so we should not overstress one at the expense of the other. Difference or affinity has no value in and of itself" (49).

Still, conceptualization of fundamental differences, especially between Asian and European or between East and West, has persisted around the world. In another paradoxical affinity, both Western and Eastern intellectuals have alleged definite opposition of Eastern and Western worldviews and belief systems, concluding that the two simply cannot understand each other. If such "inscrutability" really existed, no literary works would prevail beyond our civilizations' spatial and temporal borders: readers of a certain perspective would be unable to empathize with, or even understand, texts originating from the Other. Obviously, that has not been the case historically.

Indeed, dichotomous contrast between East and West is just fancy and mystification stemming from assumption. Specific readings and counterpointing of literary and philosophical texts from East and West do yield recognition of affinities in imagination, speculation, conception, cognition, and expression that extend beyond cultural and linguistic gaps. This recognition can promote both a better understanding of literature and international peace because people can and do perceive affinities, that is, points of mutual understanding. In *Not for Profit*, Martha C. Nussbaum recommends recognition of affinities through the belief that a simple focus on differences does not produce mutual understanding in a globalized society. Distinctions exist between East and West—but in degree, not in kind. Certainly, Eastern and Western people read and understand one another, and literary texts emerging from other civilizations' constructs can prevail across the globe—beyond linguistic, cultural, and social differences.

But for just one person to expand literary comparisons to confirm cultures' similarities is, of course, impossible. Instead, students and researchers' cooperative efforts would likely discover that authors from a broad range of regions and eras have, for instance, frequently used the same metaphors.

But how can such efforts help realize world peace? To demonstrate literature's worldwide affinity, students and researchers could compare texts from their regions with those from other regions and then post to a website the affinities in imagination, speculation, conception, cognition, and expression. New data would be compared with old, and, at minimum, students and researchers would not only contribute to literary criticism but also recognition of the world's affinity, leading to peace.

With reference to Zhang, who has contributed significantly to comparative literature and cross-cultural understanding, first in this chapter, I discuss reading literature with a suitable theoretical approach to affinity and difference. Second, I provide examples of unexpected affinities (and some differences) between cultures' literary texts. Finally, I recommend pedagogy that utilizes collaborative online international learning and an open access board.

Dichotomous View of East and West and of Self and Other

Fundamental difference between Asian and European, or East and West,[1] has long been a familiar concept to all countries' intelligentsia. For instance, in *The Geography of Thought*, the American psychologist Richard E. Nisbett alleges, "The East is a cultural Other that stands for everything that the West is not," so East and West cannot understand each other. Nisbett emphasizes a huge gap between Westerners and Asians in speculative, conceptual, and cognitive systems; he contends these differences have existed for thousands of years. As support, Nisbett presents his thinking about such fundamental differences:

---

[1] I use *the West* repeatedly, but *the West* means areas and people that have economic and political power in the international world, in other words, a kind of hegemony. As a result, in this paper, *the West* means Europe and America.

> The modern Asians, like ancient Chinese, view the world in holistic terms: They see a great deal of the field, especially background events; they are skilled in observing relationships between events; they regard the world as complex and highly changeable and its components as interrelated; they feel that control over events requires coordination with other. Modern Westerners, like the ancient Greeks, see the world in analytic, atomistic terms; they see objects as discrete and separate from their environments; they see events as moving in linear fashion when they move at all; and they feel themselves to be personally in control of events even when they are not. Not only worldviews different in a conceptual way, but also the world literally *viewed* in different ways. (108-09)

Nisbett even definitively states,

> "Hard as it is for Westerners to understand, there were only two short-lived movements of little influence in the East that shared the spirit of logical inquiry that has always been common in the West. These were *Ming jia* [Logicians] and the Mohists, or followers of Mo-tzu, both of the classical period in antiquity. (166)

Because of the fundamental differences he catalogs, Nisbett concludes that mutual understanding between Westerners and Asians cannot be expected (Nisbett 229).

Though Nisbett's statement "logical inquiry that has always been common in the West" also begs the question because logical inquiry has not "always been common in the West" – examples are Copernicus and Galileo, among many others, and the Middle Ages – some of Nisbett's many books have been translated into several languages, and his dichotomous view of the West and Asia has exerted a major influence on people worldwide. Even Sheena Iyengar, a well-known scholar on choice and a popular speaker in TED talks in the United States, relies on Nisbett's references to fundamental differences between East and West to develop arguments in *The Art of Choosing*, especially in the second chapter "Stranger in Strange Lands." For reference, in Japan, Nisbett's *The Geography of Thought* is very popular; as of July 20, 2020, the 16th impression of its first edition was in print.

Western scholars like Nisbett and Iyengar share this dichotomous view, and numerous Asian scholars have articulated a similar view. Airing his opinion about fundamental differences between East and West, the great Chinese scholar Lin Yutang clearly contrasts the Chinese, as representative of Asian peoples, with Westerners.[2] He asserts that the Chinese value practice, while Westerners emphasize reason; the Chinese value emotion, while Westerners emphasize logic; the Chinese pursue success by following heaven's will, while Westerners value objective understanding and analysis; and the Chinese value intuition and spiritual seeking, while Westerners prioritize the intellectual search for truth. Like Nesbitt, Lin concludes that these contrasts stem from fundamental differences and that East and West can never understand each other (139).

According to Lin and Nisbett's opinions, Asians do not care about logic, reasoning, objective understanding, analysis, intellectual seeking, or truth, while Westerners do not care about emotion, heaven's will, intuition, spiritual seeking, or practice. Besides all that, Nisbett states that since ancient times, neither Westerners nor Asians have changed their conceptual perspectives. Can this opinion be correct? Can such statements be true?

Zhang Longxi criticizes such conceptualization, citing varied examples and other, perhaps more persuasive, arguments. Zhang mentions that although Nisbett claims that Westerners see events moving linearly, when they move at all, the American philosopher and poet Ralph Waldo Emerson compared a life to a circle in the 1841 essay "Circles" (Zhang 39). Another famous Western (Irish) example might be W.B. Yeats's poem "The Second Coming" (1919): "Turning and turning in the widening gyre/ The falcon cannot hear the falconer;/ Things fall apart; the centre cannot hold." Yeats saw events spiraling (circling) wider and wider and then perhaps reversing to spiral narrow and narrower, in a repeated cycle. In contrast, in the essay "*Hōjōki*" (1212), or "Visions of a Torn World," as I will argue later, the thirteenth-century Japanese essayist Kaomo no Chōmei likened this world's events to a river's flow, that is, moving linearly.

Furthermore, if people from differing cultures, traditions, and social realities differ fundamentally, learning foreign languages would be pointless because, despite knowing the same words and phrases, they could not understand each other due to speculative, conceptual, and cognitive differences. Needless to say, neither could they enjoy literary works from other global regions—even in translation. Nonetheless, after reading German translations of a Persian poem and a Chinese novel, Johann Wolfgang von Goethe referred to "*Weltliteratur*" or "world literature" because literary texts, borne of regions where he had never been, so moved him. As a matter of fact, myriad literary works circulate rather freely among discrete regions, primarily in translated versions. This truth alone

---

[2] All Chinese and Japanese names, except the author's, are written in the order of "family name, first name," according to the system of writing Chinese and Japanese names.

confirms affinities of speculation and imagination in people of these supposedly oppositional civilizations, despite differences in languages, customs, traditions, cultures, and social realities. The truth is that affinity lies beyond difference and difference lies within affinity; human beings, Eastern and Western, can understand one another because of affinities beyond differences.

Zhang cites Henri Baudet, who argues that "the fundamental difference" between East and West is simply mystification stemming from fancy, not from reality (Zhang 55). Baudet further argues that Western scholars' dichotomous view emanates from imaginary association "of all sorts of images of non-Western people and worlds which flourished in our culture—images derived not from observation, experience, and perceptible reality but from a psychological urge." "That urge," Baudet continues, "creates its own realities which are totally different from the political realities," but "they are in no way subordinate in either strength or clarity since they have always possessed that absolute reality value so characteristic of the rule of the myth" (Baudet 6). A similar myth has been created in the East. In an 1987 interview with David Sexton, for instance, the Nobel Prize-winning writer Kazuo Ishiguro, who was born and lived in Nagasaki as a child but is now considered a British writer, observed, "There's a reluctance on the part of the West to think of the Japanese as human beings, and this is encouraged by the Japanese themselves who like to think that they are very different from everybody else too. Both sides are to blame for this mystification" (Sexton 31). In the dichotomous argument about culture, Eastern and Western scholars often reverse images of East and West, "so much so that whatever" they find is "very predictably the opposite" of West and East, thus always reiterating "an unfailing confirmation of fundamental cultural differences" (Zhang 41). In addition, when what scholars find is predetermined, such as Eastern and Western distinctions, their argument becomes "predictably contrastive," and they merely reaffirm their "anticipations and prejudgments rather than an observation" (Zhang 77). In fact, Nisbett states that since Asian Americans, for instance,

> have very different social experiences from those of Asians, we would expect that their perceptions and patterns of thought would resemble those of other Westerners to a substantial degree. And in fact, the perceptual patterns and reasoning styles of such participants were always intermediate between those of Asians and European Americans and sometimes were actually indistinguishable from those of European Americans. (226)

In yet another, perhaps paradoxical, affinity, we should all be calm observers with clear perspectives. With just a little independent thinking, we would realize that Lin and Nisbett's alleged dichotomous contrast between East and West cannot be accurate. In fact, comparisons of concrete textual examples from discrete Eastern and Western regions, which confirm many cross-cultural affinities, elucidate the dichotomy's inaccuracy.

Mournful Poetry and Its Linguistic Counterpoints

As a definitive argument, I begin with emotion, reason, logic, and analysis—all topics that Lin and Nisbett assert that neither Westerners nor Easterners appreciate. But of course, both Westerners and Easterners value these four concepts. Otherwise, Westerners would not read lyric (especially mournful) poetry because they do not value emotion. Nevertheless, Edgar Allan Poe, widely regarded as a central figure of American romanticism, wrote the beautiful, mournful poem "Annabel Lee" (1849) as he suffered his beloved young wife's passing. The poem begins: "It was many and many a year ago,/ In a kingdom by the sea,/ That a maiden there lived whom you may know/ By the name of Annabel Lee;/ And this maiden she lived with no other thought/ Than to love and be loved by me." The narrator's deeply felt emotion appealed to Westerners, who made the poem very popular. Japan has a similarly famous classic poem. Kakinomoto Hitomaro wrote "A Poem of Shedding Blood Tears," in *Man'youshu*. Like Poe, Kakinomoto Hitomaro suffered his beloved wife's death and wrote, "Leaving the mortal coil, we saw the elm on the bank together, by a swift flowing river." Both these poems originated from pressures of grief and anguish, have touched countless readers' hearts, and continue to be read today. Obviously both Westerners and Easterners value emotion. Besides that, poems' creation requires the fundamental affinity of poets who possess reason, logic, and analysis (to configure the poetic forms of rhyme, contrast, style, and syntax), all of which Lin and Nisbett affirmatively deny to Asian thought. Finally, Poe and Kakinomoto's poetic narrators share an unexpected affinity: imagining themselves with their beloved wives near an expanse of water, which is a basic physical and spiritual affinity for humanity.

Worldwide, many authors have written mournful poetry after experiencing suffering or misfortune, and mournful poems have strongly touched human hearts regardless of place of origin. Movahedeh Sadat Mousavi and Elham Maazallahi believe that for the well-known Iranian poet Attar Neishabouri, "the main source of love is pain: Even if you're of love, seek pain, seek pain and pain" (Mousavi and Maazallahi 14). In the research books *Is Life Only a Chorus of Happiness and Success?* and *Japanese, or People Handing Down Sorrow and Mourning* and in *Philosophy of Sorrow*, Yamaori Tetsuo and Takeuchi Seichi, respectively, cite various Japanese poems and novels to conclude that Japanese spirit and culture are characterized by sorrow and mourning. In comparing various poems from East and West, Zhang believes, "The best and the most powerful poetry touches the heart because it is produced out of the poet's painful lived experience" (*Unexpected Affinities* 55).

Additionally, and perhaps surprisingly, mournful poems considered great literature express the same metaphors across cultures and eras. Zhang introduces his respected mentor, the distinguished Chinese scholar of comparative literature Qian Zhongshu, whose persuasive line of (aptly for this argument) reasoning begins with the opinion of the great fifth-century Chinese critic Liu Xie. Liu "argues in his famous work *The Literary Mind or the Carving Dragon* that a great work of literature is often the product of the author's painful lived experience and sorrow, just 'like pearls that come out of the disease of suffering oysters'" (Qian 102, qtd. in Zhang, *From Comparison* 147). Qian then confirms that the same metaphor finds expression in *Huainan zi* (179 B.C.–122 B.C.) and in *The Analects of Confucius*. To confirm Liu's view, Qian expands the comparison to other literatures:

> Franz Grillparzer remarks that poetry is like a pearl, the product of a sick and silent shell-fish (*die Perle, das Erzeugnis des kranken stillen Muscheltieres*); Flaubert observes that a pearl is formed in the illness of the oyster (*la perle est une maladie de l'huître*), while the style of a writer flows out of a deeper sorrow (*l'écoulement d'une douleur plus profounde*). Heine wonders whether poetry is to man what the pearl is to the poor oyster, the stuff of illness that makes it suffer (*wie die Perle, die Krankheitsstoff, woran das arme Austertier leidet*). A.E. Housman maintains that poetry is a sort of "secretion; whether a natural secretion, like the turpentine in the fir, or a morbid secretion, like the pearl in the oyster." Apparently, such a metaphor is found everywhere and used by all writers independently of one another, because it expresses precisely the idea that "poetry gives vent to grievances," and that it is "produced under the pressure of suffering or misfortune." (Qian 104, qtd. in Zhang, *From Comparison* 147)

When we compare texts, we confirm an unexpected affinity of imagination across cultures and times, revealing clear evidence that Westerners and Asians' thought is not as dichotomous as Nisbett and Lin have imagined.

Philosophy and Literature

Concerning fallacies about Japanese culture, probably no one asserts an absolute inference more strongly than Samuel P. Huntington, who states in *The Clash of Civilizations and the Remaking of World Order* that no close cultural link exists between Japan and any other regions of the world. In other words, Japan has been entirely culturally isolated. As confirmed above, affinities expressed in literature reveal otherwise. However, Japanese scholars themselves often express similar misconceptions.

As a Japanese author, I now present a counterargument by evincing literary and philosophical affinities between Japan and other regions. The Japanese tend to take pride in their view of life as transient and empty; they consider *mujōkan* (the perspective of impermanence) an admirable Japanese view of life, evidencing its existence from certain literary texts, for instance, the beginning of the poetic essay *Hōjōki* by Kamo no Chōmei:

> The flowing river never stops and yet the water never stays the same.
> Foam floats upon the pools, scattering, re-forming, never lingering long.
> So it is with man and all his dwelling places here on earth. (52)

In comparing humanity (and our regions) to a flowing river, Kamo-no asserts the world's transience and change with elapsed time. We find a similar view expressed in similar terms in the epic *Metamorphoses* by the ancient Roman poet Ovid. According to Ovid, the ancient Greek Pythagoras asserted, "[T]here is nothing in the whole universe that persists. Everything flows, and is formed as a fleeting image. Time itself, also, glides, in its continual motion, no differently than a river" (Book XV: 176-98). Now, Kamo no Chōmei did not know Ovid or Pythagoras, and *vice versa*. Thus, their visions of existence are unexpectedly affinitive. In addition, *Rubā'iyāt* of the celebrated eleventh-century Persian poet Omar Khayyám expresses the world as inconstant and transient. Furthermore, Confucius describes human existence as inconstant and transient by comparing it to a flowing river: "The Master, standing by a river, said, 'It goes on like this, never ceasing day or night!'" (9:17). These examples contradict Nisbett's dichotomous view of East and West. Although Nisbett claims that in opposition to "the modern Asians" and the "ancient Chinese," "Modern Westerners, like the ancient Greeks, see the world in analytic, atomistic terms" (109), the ancient Roman Ovid, who interpreted the ancient Greek Pythagoras, sees "everything" in flow, in "continual motion," in much the same way as Kamo no Chōmei, Omar Khayyám and Confucius.

Allegedly, everything being in flow and continual motion constitutes the Japanese view of life and death, making them ambiguous so that reincarnation and eternal life are part of this incessant evanescence. The human soul is neither in heaven nor in hell; rather, it is forever becoming something else in this world. Japanese scholars repeatedly elucidate this essential principle. In *Japanese Culture*, the famous scholar of culture Umehara Takeshi claims this view forms the core of Japanese spiritual culture. Certainly, this perspective is continually expressed in Japanese literature from Sugawara no Takasue no Musume's *The Tale of Hamamatsu Chūnagon* (11 A.D.) to Mishima Yukio's *The Sea of Fertility* (1969–71) in which after death, protagonists become other beings and continue to exist in the world. Again, however, in Ovid's *Metamorphoses*, Pythagoras says:

> Everything changes, nothing dies: the spirit wanders, arriving here or there, and occupying whatever body it pleases, passing from a wild beast into a human being, from our body into a beast, but is never destroyed. As pliable wax, stamped with new designs, is no longer what it was; does not keep the same form; but is still one and the same; I teach that the soul is always the same, but migrates into different forms. (Book XV: 143-75)

In other lines, Pythagoras similarly explains the nature of a being and the world:

> Nothing keeps its own form, and Nature, the renewer of things, refreshes one shape from another. Believe me, nothing dies in the universe as a whole, but it varies and changes its aspect, and what we call "being born" is a beginning to be, of something other, than what was before, and "dying" is, likewise, ending a former state. Though, "that" perhaps is transferred here, and "this," there, the total sum is constant. (Book XV: 237-58)

Here, Ovid (or his narrator Pythagoras) presents a holistic worldview. Nisbett says that modern "Westerners, like the ancient Greeks, see the world in analytic, atomistic terms; they see objects as discrete and separate from their environments." But Ovid (or Pythagoras) sees objects as continuous and as everything; he believes that every worldly being is in unity, as Nature's configurative elements. As previously mentioned, Japanese writers—for instance, Kamo-no, Fujiwara, and Mishima—have expressed beliefs congruent with those of Ovid (or Pythagoras). To Nisbett's way of thinking, both Ovid and Pythagoras should have been Asian.

Many more examples of philosophic and literary transculture between East and West exist, but here, I briefly mention only two. First, Japanese Buddhism incorporates *hongaku* philosophy, which asserts that a Buddhist nature dwells in all beings. In other words, all human beings are by nature saved. *Hongaku* philosophy defines sin as human illusion, like a cloud or a shadow that people watch only in their minds. The West is familiar with St. Augustine's doctrine that human beings embody original sin. However, New Thought, developed under the influence of R.W. Emerson, Phineas P. Quimby, and others in the nineteenth-century United States, holds that divinity dwells within every person. From a Christian-centric viewpoint, this thought is frequently alleged to be heterodoxic, but, regarding human nature, it resembles *hongaku* philosophy. Second, "*carpe diem*" or "seize the day" is well-known through Horace's phrase "*Carpe diem quam minimum credula postero*" in his *Odes* (Book I. 11), in which he insisted that a wise person is not concerned about the distant future but lives today, in the here and now, in fleeting human life (52). Horace's *carpe diem* exerted substantial influence on Western authors. The seventeenth-century British Cavalier poet Robert Herrick wrote the famous line "Gather ye rosebuds while ye may" in his 1648 poem "To the Virgins, To Make Much of Time," and the twentieth-century American Nobel Prize-winning novelist Saul Bellow wrote *Seize the Day* (1956) in which a character says, "Seize the day" to the protagonist who struggles with life, just waiting for help or good luck. Similarly, in *Essays in Idleness* (1330–32?), the Japanese poet and essayist Yoshida Kenkō insisted on the importance of living in the here and now. In chapter 108, he observes, "No one begrudges the passing moment. Is this because they are wise, or because they are fools? [...] [O]ne dedicated to the way must not concern himself over the distant future. His only care should be not to let the present moment slip vainly through his fingers." In chapter 92, moreover, Yoshida argues:

> A man engaged in Buddhist practice will tell himself at night that there is always the morning, or in the morning will anticipate the night, always intending to make more effort later. And if such are your days, how much less aware must you be of a passing moment's indolence. Why should it be so difficult to carry something out right now when you think of it, to seize the instant? It is said to be born from the perspective of impermanence.

In the writings of Horace, Herrick, Bellow, and Yoshida "Seize the instant" and "Seize the day" are equivalent and common, existing beyond gaps among Greek thought, Christianity, and Buddhism.

On Stylistic and Cognitive Limits

So far, I have argued human beings' affinity in imagination, conception, and worldview beyond visible differences in culture, language, and tradition by citing specific, diverse texts. Although Zhang refers to "the consensus of cognitive scientists about some general commonality among all human beings" (*From Comparison* 37), I mention in this section the cognitive and stylistic limits of reading both original and translated texts.

So long as Easterners and Westerners have affinities in speculative, conceptual, and cognitive systems, I can assert translatability between regions' literary works. However, few others are likely to read a translated text very similarly to a native speaker of the original language. For one thing, certain differences, such as the grammatical gender of many European languages, cause translators' difficulty in capturing, absolutely accurately, the original text's form and style. In *Literary Women*, Ellen Moers notes that celebrated French women writers, such as Anne Louise Germaine de Staël, George Sand, and Simone Weil, intentionally choose grammatical gender when they express oppression of female agency and represent the self-consciousness of sex. For instance, for a love scene, French authors can write female and masculine nouns in alternative order, like *personne* (person; feminine), *cœur* (heart;

masculine), *âme* (soul; feminine), and *esprit* (mind; masculine). However, such an expressive effect disappears in texts translated into Asian or other languages (including English) without grammatical gender. Similarly, when reading a text translated from an Asian to a European language, a Western reader may find meaning not conveyed by the original. I take the indefinite article as an example. Essentially, Asian languages do not include articles, the lack of which affects a literary text's meaning in translation. A well-known example is Matsuo Bashō's "*Kawazu*" ("Frog") *haiku* (a 17-syllable poem): *Furu ike ya/ kawazu tobikomu/ mizu no oto*. Donald Kean translated the poem: "The ancient pond/ A frog leaps in/ The sound of the water," while Lafcadio Hearn imagined plural frogs: "Old pond–frogs jumped in–sound of water." The number of frogs affects the sound of water that readers hear in their minds, but the point lies not in which translation is correct, but in that readers may freely imagine the water's sound without an indefinite article preceding the Japanese noun "*kawazu*." In contrast, translation requiring an indefinite article hinders readers' imaginative power. Similarly, differences in lexical connotations also change an original text into another, perhaps independent work. For instance, in the last scene of Bernard Friot's "*Personne*" (2007) in *Histoires Presses*, a story for children, the narrator regards his or her own figure in the bathroom mirror. The narrative ends with one word, "*Personne*," which has a deconstructive, double image: "*personne*" means "a person" but also "no one." If *personne* cannot be translated with a word that encompasses the double image, the story becomes a different narrative.

Apart from translation, linguistic cognition—of symbol and metaphor—and reading mode also affect readers' understanding, even in the reading of an original text. For instance, Suzuki Akiyoshi refers to discrete interpretations of F. Scott Fitzgerald's novel *The Great Gatsby* by his Japanese, American, Chinese, and Korean students. Japanese students tend to read the novel as a story of pure love. American students interpret it as an account of the American dream or as a story about female gender oppression. Some Chinese and Korean students criticize it for its portrayal of illicit love and thus cannot accept it. For them, *Gatsby* concerns ethics, perhaps shaped by their Confucian thought. In contrast, Japanese students, who live where Confucianism is not as influential as previously, notice Gatsby's single-minded passion for Daisy. Americans, who value self-actualization in a capitalistic society, attend more to class identity and to liberation from gender-based oppression. Which is the right interpretation and which is not cannot be asserted. As David Damrosch states, "[W]hen a text goes beyond a national border, the text itself transforms" (281)."

A Persian poem and a Chinese novel impressed Goethe, recalling *Weltliteratur*. However, he could not have responded to these works in a manner identical with Persian or Chinese readers, respectively, because translations into German could not fully capture original form and style. Additionally, an original text changes depending on a reader's linguistic, intellectual, and socio-cultural contexts. Indeed, according to Jacques Lacan, the agency of "I" is structured by *le symbolique*. In addition, the brain scientist Antonio Damasio asserts, "[e]motion, feeling, and biological regulation all play a role in human reasoning" (8). Humans can feel something and thus think of it; they can think of something and thus feel it, but they express both feeling and thought in language.

Even so, varied responses to a literary text do not imply the impossibility of understanding the text; neither do they signify a literary text's failure to transcend cultures. Certainly, completely representing an entire text in translation is not possible, but to foster improved understanding, a translator can add notes or employ thick translation. Still, a literary text itself, to some degree, accepts several interpretations. As Umberto Eco remarks on textual intention in *Interpretation and Overinterpretation*, a word should and can be understood within the whole structure of the text. As Zhang emphasizes, the text does not change, but "the reader's initial conjecture is continually adjusted and modified so that a more adequate understanding may arise in the process of reading." (*Allegoresis* 126). This feat is also possible through discussion by readers who read a text within its whole structure from multidimensional viewpoints. As previously mentioned, Japanese, American, Chinese, and Korean students responded differently to *The Great Gatsby*, but none read it as a happy story or merely criticized Gatsby. However, they unanimously empathized with Gatsby's loss of love and censured those who benefited from Gatsby but failed to attend his funeral. Besides that, all the students, despite having read from multidimensional viewpoints, understood each interpretation and achieved adequate understanding of the novel.

Such understanding is possible because of affinities that transcend diverse readers' linguistic and cultural gaps. Indeed, when we read a poem or a story about a beloved person's death, it evokes sadness, not laughter, and we can share that sadness with others. Furthermore, a novel in which people do not mourn a man's early death, despite their indebtedness to him, evokes our anger and pity, not appreciation. We can and do share problems. Empathy with pure love or single-minded passion, strife in attaining a dream, resistance to oppression of agency, understanding of illicit love's immorality: these are common to all humankind. People in the East and the West are not so fundamentally different that they cannot understand each other; they are, rather, affinitive in imagination, concept, worldview, and feeling in ways that transcend differences of culture, language, and tradition. Therefore, a literary text can surpass cultural and social dissimilarities to be (more than) adequately understood by readers across civilizations.

Pedagogy

People tend to draw arbitrary boundaries between affinity and disparity, so we need particular texts to confirm speculative, conceptual, and cognitive similarities *and* differences. Comparison of literary texts, especially specific examples, clearly demonstrates affinity across civilizations and eras—in human imagination, speculation, conception, cognition, and expression. Of course, affinity does not mean ultimate sameness, and particular examples frequently evidence significant differences. However, readers' understanding of dissimilarity itself signifies familiarity with each comparative disparity. Otherwise, readers would fail to perceive differences. Indeed, as long as the reader is familiar with two compared aspects, their difference is not unfathomable.

Difference cannot exist without affinity and, of course, affinity does not exist without specifics. Importantly, finding specific affinities in globally varied texts refutes ethnocentrism—here, Orientalism and Occidentalism—and can promote peace. Moreover, finding difference suitably leads to respect for diversity. Indeed, reading widely varied literary texts can contribute to better understanding of literature itself and of humanity, thus promoting peace in the world.

In a project of literary comparison, students will surely realize the value of their presentations to the world, especially since understanding all languages is impossible. Some students might present affinities among certain literary texts in French, English, and Japanese to other students who understand French, English, and Chinese. The latter students explain affinities to the former, and, consequently, they all understand affinities in French, English, Chinese, and Japanese texts. If students continue studying literature with diverse partners, they gradually come to comprehend literature itself, know more about various countries and regions, and understand human beings better as a whole.

However, just one person expanding comparisons of world literature and confirming authors' views, has its limitations. Thus, students (and researchers as well) should cooperate on such a project. Currently, most colleges enroll many international students as part of globalization's rapid progression. In such diverse and cooperative classrooms, international students can compare texts from their regions with those from other regions.

If a class of students lacks diversity, however, a teacher can form a joint class in which students in other courses or other colleges enroll. If a course joins another, two types are conceivable: 1) a joint class in which an Anglophone literature course collaborates with another in which various international students enroll; 2) a joint class in which an Anglophone literature course collaborates with a course offering other regions' literature. Additionally, a teacher can form yet another type of joint class that consists of his/her course and another course in another college in the same or another country. To work with a college in another country, teachers can and should establish an online portal community between regions and/or countries. Doing so through a social networking service, such as Facebook, would be useful because it offers a community where teachers worldwide can search for a partner school according to time-zone differences, students' academic ability, suitable class periods, and other criteria. Teachers can access the community laboratory, connect with one another, design lesson plans, and identify useful classroom tools and materials. However, finding a college and forming an international joint class can be much easier when a teacher refers to colleges with which his/her college has an academic cooperation agreement and/or student exchange. Besides that, a joint class can help prepare groups of students for study abroad.

For joint classes, the ideal would be for both student groups to meet consistently, learn literature collaboratively, and conduct all discussions together. However, that is difficult. More practically, groups of students should first study separately and conduct discussions during only a fourth or a fifth of all classes in each course in a semester or in a quarter; otherwise students can hardly settle down to read and study a literary text. For example then, in three or four consecutive classes, American literature students read R. W. Emerson's *Essays*, especially "Circles," and Japanese literature students read Haruki Murakami's short novels, especially "Circle." At the fourth or fifth class (the first joint meeting), students explain these works to each other and discuss their affinities and differences. Students frequently believe that American or Western thinking is linear and Japanese or Eastern thinking is circular; therefore, affinities between works by Emerson, or what is called the "American mind," and by Murakami, who learned the Japanese mind from his father, a Buddhist priest, might surprise students and expand their horizons. With that new knowledge, next, for three or four weeks, American literature students read Henry David Thoreau's *Walden*, a nature-writing text, and Japanese literature students read ancient travel writings, including *haiku* (Japanese poems of 17 syllables), for instance, Matsuo Bashō's *Narrow Road to the Deep North*. Then, in the second joint class, students explain these texts to each other and discuss affinities and differences, for instance, in metaphor, color, and sound illustrating nature and criticism of human society. The discussion would lead the students to finding in both texts a view that a human being is a part of nature, and open their eyes to the fact that such a view is common to the Eastern and Western worlds. To deepen their study, students should record their findings in a blog post or Google Document. Expressing their findings' culmination can effectively solidify their knowledge, engage them more deeply, and stimulate their minds.

For students in each course to read comparable novels and then discuss affinities and differences in three or four consecutive joint classes is also valuable. For instance, French literature students read Jules Michelet's *La Sorcière*, and Japanese literature students read Murakami Haruki's *Norwegian Wood*. In Murakami's novels, a dead female character often and repeatedly overlaps other women. Michelet also overlaps a witch with many witches – a technique that stems from some professional and/or sad experiences. He wrote *La Sorcière* after his wife died and soon thereafter, his girlfriend. As Jean Giono notes, from Michelet's reading of ancient writings or from listening to the voices of the dead as head of the National Archives' Historical Section, and from losing both beloved women in swift succession, he might have found an eternal life beyond death, that no person ever dies, or that human beings are unified in an eternal project described in each human body.[3] In addition to overlapping women, Michelet was interested in the waterfront and the sea as places of life and unity, as in *La Mer*. In this point, too, Michelet's texts are similar to Murakami's, where characters who lost their sweethearts walk on the border between the ground and the sea.[4] Hence, students can find in them various affinities (and differences).

As another example, comparison of narrative between modern twentieth-century Anglophone literature, such as Virginia Woolf's *Mrs. Dalloway*, James Joyce's *Ulysses*, and William Faulkner's *The Sound and the Fury* and *As I Lay Dying*, and tenth- and eleventh-century Japanese texts, such as Izumi Shikibu's *Diary*, Sugawara no Takasue no Musume's *Sarashina Diary*, and Fujiwara no Michitsuna no Haha's *The Gossamer Years*, would make students surprisedly find a stream of consciousness in them.[5] Reading Walter Pater's *Marius the Epicurean*, Homer's (alleged) *Odysseus*, and *The Kojiki, or Records of Ancient Matters (of Japan)*, would lead students to find affinities in a metaphor of life and soul as a (white) bird. Other examples may be found in Zhang Longxi's books *Unexpected Affinities* and *From Comparison to World Literature*, which include various examples of affinities *in* differences, especially those among Chinese, Anglophone, and European literatures. These comparisons could surely suggest ideas for a syllabus and trigger comparison and discussion among students from varying regions.

---

[3] Shinoda, Koichi. "Kaisetsu" ["Exposition"], in *Majo*, vol. 1, or a Japanese version of Jules Michelet's *La Sorcière*, translated by Shinoda (Tokyo: Iwanami, 1983), p. 316.
[4] See Akiyoshi Suzuki, "Mapping the Subterranean of Haruki Murakami's Literary World," *IAFOR Journal of Literature & Librarianship*, 2(1) (2013): pp. 17–42.
[5] Stream of consciousness in ancient Japanese literature was found by the Japanese scholar Doi Kōchi.

For global students to read a text at the same time, like *The Great Gatsby* as mentioned earlier, a good example is John Steinbeck's *Of Mice and Men* because, in my experience, affinity and difference in reading modes are interesting. After explaining the Depression era as the background of *Of Mice and Men* and students have read it, the teacher should ask questions like "What do you think brought about the final incident?", "What do you feel about the story's ending?", "What do you think of George Milton?", "If you were Lennie, what would you feel in the last scene?" and "If you were George and saw Lennie about to be shot, what would you think and what would you do?" Basically, students tend to be moved by the story, often mentioning similar issues, such as friendship, loyalty, endurance, suppression of the weak, and impressions. However, some Japanese men feel nothing about the final scene, insisting it unworthy of special mention because they see the murder as a matter of course: a man of *Samurai* or chivalrous spirit can kill his friend because their relationship is important and strong or because he does not want his friend killed by an enemy or a stranger. Naturally then, George chivalrously protects his best friend Lennie. Some Japanese students even criticize the final scene as savage because it typifies Japanese gangsters' behavior in films. Some female students—Japanese and American—note the strangeness of a world of men, focusing on identity; the final scene is a tragedy brought about by the homosocial community. Students in developing countries, and some Japanese and American, criticize capitalism, regarding George and Lennie as victims of the economic system.

In the class of *The Great Gatsby*, the teacher should ask students as follows: "What do you think of Gatsby's effort to win back Daisy's love?", "If you were Daisy, what would you think about Gatsby's behavior?", "If you were Gatsby, what would you do when Daisy refuses you?", "If the story of Gatsby were set in your hometown, what would you think of Gatsby's behavior?", "What do you think of people's morals in Gatsby's neighborhood?" As mentioned earlier, students would tell their own opinions, unconsciously based on their own culture, find affinities and differences and discuss their cross-cultural reading seriously and enjoyably.

In joint classes where students cannot be together physically, they can discuss via Zoom, Microsoft Teams, and other collaboration platforms.[6] Of course, teachers must consider time-zone differences, suitable class periods, and other criteria. In addition to Zoom-type discussions or if time-zone or

---

[6] Collaborative Online International Learning (COIL) is helpful for a joint global class. For detailed information about COIL, see the website of the American Council on Education (https://www.acenet.edu/Programs-Services/Pages/Communities/US-Japan-COIL-Initiative.aspx).

academic calendar differences do not ensure sufficient time for joint classes, students can compare texts and write results as new or additional information, for instance, in a Google Document. Comparison of new to old data would contribute to literary knowledge and, more significantly, to knowledge of global humanity. The Google Document will surely be a valuable collaborative research paper. Students' short presentations of findings, with self-introduction by VoiceThread before the first joint class, are also useful and stimulating, and work well for icebreaking.

In short, students from various regions study literature and mutually illuminate their findings at several planned meetings during an academic term. Such collaborative classes can contribute to better understanding of literature and of human beings, and promote peace in the world.

Bibliography

The Analects of Confucius [Lunyu]. "Zi nan." Translated by A. Charles Muller. Retrieved on January 21, 2021, from http://www.acmuller.net/con-dao/analects.html#div-10.

Baudet, Henri. *Paradise on Earth: Some Thoughts on European Images of Non-European Man*, trans. Elizabeth Wenthold. Middletown, CT: Wesleyan University Press, 1988.

Damasio, Antonio R. *Descartes' Error: Emotion, Reason, and the Human Brain*. New York, NY: Penguin, 2005. Rept.

Damrosch, David. *What Is World Literature?* Princeton, NJ: Princeton University Press, 2003.

Doi, Kōchi. *History of Eastern and Western Cultures: Dialogue with Doi Kōchi [Tōzaibunka no nagare——Doi Kōchi taidanshū]*. Tokyo: Kenkyūsha, 1973.

———. *Tradition and Communication of Literature [Bungaku no dentō to kōryū]*. Tokyo: Iwanami Shoten, 1964.

Eco, Umberto, with R. Rorty, J. Culler, & C. Brooke-Rose. *Interpretation and Overinterpretation*. S. Collimi (Ed.). Cambridge: Cambridge University Press, 1992.

Friot, Bernard. *Histoires Presses*. Paris: Milan, 2007.

Herrick, Robert. "To the Virgins, To Make Much Time." In Thomas Bailey Aldrich (Ed.), *Poems of Robert Herrick: A Selection from Hesperides and Noble Numbers*, with an introduction by Thomas Bailey Aldrich. New York, NY: The Century, 1900, p. 54.

Horace. *Ad Leuconoën*. In William Lee, *Translations in English Verse from Ovid, Horace, Tacitus, etc*. London: Rivingtons, Waterloo Place, 1860, p. 52.

Huntington, Samuel. P. *The Clash of Civilizations and the Remaking of World Order*. New York, NY: Simon & Schuster, 1996.

Iyengar, Sheena. *The Art of Choosing*. New York, NY: Twelve, 2011.

Kakinomoto, Hitomaro. "A Poem of Shedding Blood Tears" ["Ryūketsu aidō ka"]. In Satake Akihiro et al. (Eds.), *Man'youshu*, Book II. Tokyo: Iwanami Shoten, 2000, pp. 210–212.

Kamo no, Chōmei. *Visions of a Torn World* [*Hōjōki*], trans. Moriguchi Yasuhiro and David Jenkins. Tokyo: IBC Publishing, 2012.
Lin, Yutang. *Chinese Humor*, trans. S. Yoshimura. Tokyo: Iwanami Shinsho, 1982.
Michaels, Walter Benn. *The Shape of the Signifier: 1967 to the End of History.* Princeton, NJ: Princeton University Press, 2004.
―――. *The Trouble with Diversity: How We Learned to Love Identity and Ignore Inequality.* New York: Holt, 2006.
Moers, Ellen. *Literary Women.* New York, NY: Doubleday, 1976.
Mousavi, Movahedeh Sadat and Elham Maazallahi. "A Literary Comparison between the Canonization and Reckless Butterfly." *Annals of Language and Literature*, 3 (1) (2019): 12–17.
Nisbett, Richard. E. *The Geography of Thought.* New York, NY: Free Press, 2004.
Nussbaum, Martha C. *Not for Profit: Why Democracy Needs the Humanities.* Princeton, NJ: Princeton University Press, 2010.
Ovid. *Metamorphosis*, trans. A. S. Klein. In *The Ovid Collection*, 2000. Retrieved July 2, 2019, from http://ovid.lib.virginia.edu/trans/Metamorph15.htm.
Poe, Edger Allan. "Annabel Lee." In D. Edmund (Ed.), *The Poetical Works of Edgar Allan Poe.* New York, NY: George H. Doran, 1921, pp. 23–26.
Qian, Zhongshu. *Collection of Seven Essays.* Shanghai: Shanghai guji, 1985.
Sexton, David. "Interview: David Sexton meets Kazuo Ishiguro" (1987). In Brian W. Shaffer and Cynthia F. Wong (Eds.), *Conversations with Kazuo Ishiguro*, Jackson, MI: University Press of Mississippi, 2008, pp. 27–34.
Shinoda, Koichi. "Kaisetsu" ["Exposition"]. In *Majo*, vol. 1, or a Japanese version of Jules Michelet's *La Sorcière*, translated by Shinoda. Tokyo: Iwanami, 1983, pp. 301–25.
Suzuki, Akiyoshi. "How Should We Read Literature from a Certain Area from the Viewpoints of Other Language-speaking Areas?" *The IAFOR Journal of Literature and Librarianship*, 3 (1) (2014): 9–39.
―――. "Mapping the Subterranean of Haruki Murakami's Literary World." *IAFOR Journal of Literature & Librarianship*, 2(1) (2013): pp. 17–42.
Takeuchi, Sēichi. *Philosophy of Sorrow: On the Roots of Japanese Spiritual History* [*"Kanashimi" no tetsugaku――Nihon seishinshi no Minamoto wo saguru*]. Tokyo: NHK Books, 2009.
Umehara, Takeshi. *On Japanese Culture* [*Nihon bunka ron*]. Tokyo: Kodansha, 1976.
Yamaori, Tetsuo. *Is Life Only a Chorus of Happiness and Success?: The History of Japanese Spirit of Sorrow* [*Kōfuku to seikō dake ga jinsei ka――"Kanashimi" no nihon seishinshi*]. Kyoto: PHP, 2007.
Yamaori, Tetsuo and Takashi Saitō. *Japanese, or People Handing Down Sorrow and Mourning* [*"Kanashimi" wo kataritsugu nihonjin*]. Kyoto: PHP, 2003.
Yeats, William Butler. "The Second Coming." *W. B. Yeats: Selected Poetry*, ed. by A. Norman Jeffares. London: Macmillan, 1968, pp. 99–100.
Yoshida, Kenkō. *Kenkō and Chōmei: Essays in Idleness and Hōjōki*, trans. M. McKinney. New York, NY: Penguin, 2013. Kindle.
Zhang, Longxi. *Allegoresis: Reading Canonical Literature East and West.* Ithaca, NY: Cornell University Press, 2005.

———. *From Comparison to World Literature.* New York, NY: SUNY, 2015.
———. *Unexpected Affinities: Reading across Cultures.* Toronto: University of Toronto Press, 2007.

Chapter 4
DEI, NDAs, and the Value of Literature: Dismantling Educational Privilege with Nontraditional Assignments

Melissa Ryan
Alfred University

Abstract

Melissa Ryan's (Alfred University) "DEI, NDAs, and the Value of Literature" seeks to validate students' unique contributions in creating a web resource for future learners. In contextualizing this project, she articulates concerns about the relationship between traditional literary analysis assignments and educational privilege, seeing disposable assignments as in some cases more than a missed opportunity. Reflecting on the capacity of nondisposable assignments to address diversity, equity, and inclusion goals, as well as to make the value of literature more available to all students, she shares lessons learned from some preliminary steps toward rethinking literature assignments.

Keywords: Diversity, Equity, and Inclusion (DEI), nontraditional writing assignments, multicultural literature, pedagogy

***

Literature courses – mine, at least – are typically set up to reward students for fluency in a certain kind of writing: thesis-driven analytical arguments with paragraphs carefully structured around textual evidence. This is to some degree desirable, since the institutional imperatives embedded in this kind of academic discourse reflect our core values, like evidence-based reasoning and critical thinking. But these essay assignments may effectively exclude students who haven't already internalized the model; that is, they are more likely to show who's good at school than who's responding to literature in a meaningful way. The question I would like to explore here is what role nondisposable assignments (NDAs) can play in addressing the marginalization of students without that institutional fluency – that is, in advancing the goals of diversity, equity, and inclusion (DEI) – and in accessing more of the value of literature for all students.

It's worth noting as a kind of preamble that the purpose or value of literature courses as distinct from composition can be difficult to elucidate. Because general education literature and first year composition are often almost indistinguishable – I think my institution is pretty typical in presenting the second semester of a two-semester introductory sequence as writing primarily about literature – I tend to approach writing assignments in literature classes through the lens of comp studies. This isn't a bad thing, since composition has such well developed resources, but the teaching of literature specifically feels relatively underconceptualized; I have self-scrutiny to a Puritanical degree, but this doesn't necessarily amount to a literature pedagogy.[1] Although I spend a lot of time thinking about the value of general education literature courses, I often continue to assign a traditional thesis-driven literary analysis as the formal (hence "real") work of these courses. This form feels like something I inherited without much consideration of what literature is for or what I want students to do with the experience or how I could use writing assignments to help them do it. As Sherry Linkon points out, "course design usually emphasizes content knowledge – what we want students to understand about literature, rather than what we want them to be able to do with literature" (70). So I focus my attention on what we'll read in what order – planning content, even though only one of my learning outcomes has to do with content, and constructing writing assignments assuming that 4-5 double-spaced pages exploring a theme or pattern of representation is a natural and necessary thing to produce.

I'm also aware of what feels like increasingly cross purposes – a gap between why this gen ed literature course is required, and why I think it's worth taking.[2] Some of this is driven by the assessment framework: sincerity may be hard to gauge, but I can more readily measure a student's ability to support a claim, develop an argument, articulate a why or a so what. And these are valuable skills – but they're not necessarily why we read fiction or poetry, or at least not a cause for the love of reading, though they may be effects. My standard course overview talks about quality of life – my syllabus tells students our larger purpose is "to become more alive, more aware, more empathetic deep-thinking humans" – but my learning outcomes can't (I'd like to know if they turn out to be good people who live deliberately, but the longitudinal data aren't available

---

[1] See Paul T. Corrigan on "comp envy," the hope that "the impressive body of pedagogical knowledge and practice that writing studies has developed might inspire productive envy among teachers of literature" (417).
[2] On the question of value, see especially Cristina Vischer Bruns, *Why Literature? The Value of Literary Reading and What It Means for Teaching*.

to me). From an institutional perspective, describing our work strictly in terms of textual analysis has its advantages; I'd rather define the requirement in terms of how we read so I can make my own decisions about what we read. But if the formal assignments reflect only a particular kind of analysis – a kind that comes pretty naturally to me but may not to all of them – then the work may misrepresent, or only partially represent, what the course is actually about or trying to do.

It's interesting to me that even my attempts to incorporate more of their relationship to the text into the literary analysis essay don't seem to have much of an effect on the final form. I invite personal narrative – usually in some self-contained way, like in the introduction or conclusion, so they don't have to worry about dulling the analytical edge of close reading – but often students just don't do it, like they don't trust the guidelines. I speculate that many students are just trying to replicate the form they were taught (no "I"!) and so aren't ready to take chances. But in truth, they could also be responding to the values embedded in my course design. Without thinking about the implications, I typically put meaningful activities into low-stakes reflection papers (read Emerson, and then go outside and see like a child; read Scott Russell Sanders's "Buckeye," and then draw the map of a place that you love), but what earns the real points are exams and formal textual analysis, where the grade distribution tends to reflect formal writing skills they did or did not bring with them. (Am I worried that my grades won't fall into a bell curve if they've all got an equal shot at an A? Am I anxious about academic rigor, and leaning on formal academic essays as a proxy for it? These are uncomfortable but necessary questions.)

Ideally, I'd like to detach grades from purpose or value, but students who've spent 12 and more years in a work-for-points economy have certain expectations – and I've internalized them myself. I look, for example, at a sequence of events from my last Multicultural American Lit syllabus. We watched Elizabeth Acevedo's TEDx MidAtlantic talk, "I use my poetry to confront violence against women," in which she offers the recitation of poetry as an expression of hope. I then asked students to memorize and recite a poem for the class, as a homework assignment Acevedo had given them (she had directed her audience to find a woman poet and memorize one of her pieces, and on a day when gender oppression feels like too much, recite that poem). This was a day I loved, especially for the student (an underperformer, disengaged) who recited a poem of her own composition. But this activity was attached to no points or grade, which felt vaguely exploitative, like I'd asked for unpaid labor. A formal essay worth 15% of the final grade was due the day after the poetry recitation, sending a pretty clear message: the least original assignment is what counts, and the process of finding a poem and learning it by heart – the thing that really counts – doesn't make it into the final reckoning.

And so we keep on like this: they write this thesis-driven analytical essay for the grade, I agonize over comments they mostly either don't read or can't make use of, and then the essay gets thrown away – along with all our work. These are what David Wiley has called "disposable assignments": their sole purpose is to demonstrate skill, and the sole motivation for most students is the grade. As Wiley has written, not only do they "add no value to the world," but "they suck value out of the world" because of the time spent writing and grading something that will be thrown away ("What is Open Pedagogy?"). As the fatigue across campus at the semester's end reveals, we exhaust ourselves going through the motions.

In general, the disposable assignment could be characterized as a missed opportunity, approximately 2 billion hours a semester (according to Wiley et al's estimate in "A Preliminary Exploration") that could be put to better use. But for some students and in certain courses, it feels more damaging. Teaching discussion-based, student-centered courses, especially at an institution like mine that is able to cap such classes at 20-25, gives us a unique opportunity – or maybe something more, something like responsibility – to develop relationships with students. Because of the things we tend to talk about in literature classes, we may be more able to see the student as an individual, to hear more of who they are and what they think, than might be possible in Chemistry or Math. This is particularly important for students who fall through other cracks, students who are more likely to be suffering what Cia Verschelden calls "bandwidth loss," the cognitive burden of navigating various kinds of psychological threats due to racial, ethnic, or socioeconomic status. Marginalized students at a predominantly white academic institution are more likely to encounter "microaggression, stereotype threat, belongingness uncertainty, and other sociopsychological underminers, so named because when they are part of lived reality, they act to undermine and diminish cognitive capacity" (6). Our courses in the Social Justice Studies program, including my course in Multicultural American Literature, often attract a higher percentage of such students. In the face of an unfamiliar and in some cases seemingly hostile environment, these students may be looking for a course that validates, or at least resonates with, their identities and home communities. If they take a class like Multicultural American Lit looking for connection with their experience, and I ask them to do something with their reading experience that feels purposeless or alien, the missed opportunity is more troubling.

Success in academic essays of the disposable type is more likely to reflect familiarity with academic conventions than authentic engagement with a text. There's a certain confidence and polish, a kind of AP quality, that inevitably earns an A, especially at the general education level. But for some students, the traditional essay form – like the (predominantly white) college campus – may not feel like a place they belong. Defining academic discourse as "the specific yet tacit discursive style expected of participants in the academy," White and Lowenthal argue that these "tacit codes" deepen structural inequities; college instructors expect students to have internalized analytical essay conventions at some earlier point, but "not all K-12 students receive the same access to or have the same motivation for learning and appropriating academic literacy" (White and Lowenthal 284). Further, students may actively resist a discourse they may perceive as "monolinguistic, homogenous, and sometimes hegemonic" (287); students who are already a little ambivalent about what it means to be book smart may refuse to code-switch.[3]

Rewarding institutional fluency seems to be particularly at odds with the ethos of a class like Multicultural Lit. There are, as Alexander and Rhodes point out in "Flattening Effects: Composition's Multicultural Imperative and the Problem of Narrative Coherence," many homogenizing forces in the classroom, especially if the classroom population replicates the institution. Dominant culture students may resist the recognition of difference, may overwrite real inequities in an effort to identify universal human themes. "Multicultural pedagogies frequently rely on narratives of inclusion, which often seek to contain difference in order to make it legible, identifiable, and thus acceptable to a normative readership" (431). Institutional culture, including academic discourse, may be yet another homogenizing force, causing everyone to perform similar kinds of moves and putting everyone in the same relationship to the text: distanced, objective, academic. The attempt in a class like Multicultural Lit to be disruptive on the level of content – to question dominant narratives of Americanness – may be undermined on the level of form.

This dilemma reminds me of "Aria," Richard Rodriguez's classic essay about bilingual education, one of the readings for the Multicultural Lit class that always generates a lot of discussion. Distinguishing between what he initially experiences as the private language of familial intimacy and the public language of the institution, he argues for the necessity of linguistic exile. But although the essay insists that intimacy is ultimately embedded in relationships, not in a particular language, the sense of loss remains profound: a kind of death, in the metaphor linking his grandmother's face at her funeral with the

---

[3] Synthesizing a number of studies, White and Lowenthal define the core elements of the university discourse: "Verbal assertiveness and voluntary participation, formality and explicitness, binary agonism, objectivity, specialized jargon, elements of display, and selectivity" (297). They argue that "Each of these components of academic discourse is unique, and almost all of them are based on White, Western linguistic norms" which "are largely foreign to many minority students" and in some cases "run completely counter to specific cultural linguistic/discursive norms" (297).

public face – purposefully arranged, unnatural, institutional – the nonnative speaker deploys in an English-speaking environment. "Her face appeared calm – but distant and unyielding to love. It was not the face I remembered seeing most often. It was the face she made in public when the clerk at Safeway asked her some question and I would have to respond. It was her public face the mortician had designed with his dubious art" (Rodriguez 328). Traditional essays often strike me as similarly lifeless, resembling (as if by mortician's art) in some way what I've described in the assignment, but mostly a public face, desperately trying to avoid the first person because somebody told them that was the rule, a more or less coerced attempt to transact some business in a language I speak and they don't. Reflecting on the "hollowness" of student work – as Sheridan Blau puts it, students "behave as if they are obliged to hunt for symbols,... engage in perfunctory discussions of prescribed universal themes, or gratuitously compare and contrast characters, rather than address any of the issues that might illuminate a text for a reader who cares about it or account for why a text might be important or interesting or even offensive to real readers" (qtd. in Bruns 3) – Cristina Vischer Bruns describes students engaged in "mechanical tasks," devoid of the emotional investment that would make the work meaningful. Similarly, Sherry Lee Linkon draws the analogy of language fluency – experts are like native speakers of literary language, and students are second language learners (6). In "Aria," Rodriguez demonstrates the necessity of achieving fluency in the public language; with the language of literary analysis, that necessity is not so clear.

What this all amounts to is my hope that disrupting disposable assignments may expose more fundamental sources of value in literary study – and in so doing, may empower the students who are disenfranchised by existing institutional models. For one thing, rethinking assignment structures can empower marginalized students by shifting focus from deficits to what education theorists call "funds of knowledge," the benefits of family and community life that students bring to the classroom. The life experiences that may be linked to academic disadvantage in some situations are a real advantage, a source of unique expertise, when it comes to making sense of literature. Writing assignments explicitly built on this expertise may remove some barriers to engagement. As Cia Verschelden writes, "When we see students' values and life experiences as funds of knowledge that contribute to their learning, we affirm each of the students, and by connecting new material to what they already know, we cooperate with the way their brain prefers to function. In this way, we increase the likelihood that students will feel a sense of belonging and that their learning will be enhanced" (Verschelden 84). As a further step, open pedagogy advocates point toward a radical reconceptualization of skills assessment. Nondisposable assignments – asking not just for different kinds of writing but doing different things with it – rethink both the purpose and the audience; instead of being for the instructor and for the grade, NDAs may be more truly student-centered, and as such may be a way to address some of these questions of equity. By "interrogating and dismantling systems that perpetuate oppression and centering the experiences of those with historically marginalized identities," Seraphin et al argue, "NDAs may level the playing field for students from systematically disadvantaged or socially marginalized groups" (Seraphin et al 87).

I don't have a concrete answer to the questions I've raised; I'm not going to detail the superassignment that inspires lifelong passion for reading and distributes As to all the right people. But I will describe a couple of easily adaptable experiments I've undertaken with these objectives in mind, part of a larger process of introspection about how I can make my courses most useful for the diverse students we find in our classrooms. The first assignment revision, in my Multicultural American Lit class, began with my lament that the formal essays never quite live up to what I think we've achieved in class discussion. There are those days when the room is energized and awake, we're discovering something about the text and the world, and I look forward to reading the papers that follow – only to find the same range of too rough to too safe, the same reheated high school essay. I thought that changing the form might forestall whatever impulse siphons the life from their ideas when they're committed to paper.

Discussion in multicultural literature classrooms in particular draws much of its life from the various backgrounds and perspectives students bring. This is perhaps always true when we're talking about literature, but we're here in many cases talking about experiences that are underrepresented in and undervalued by the dominant culture. Our readings are new-canonical and non-canonical; we talk about what happens when outsider knowledge is validated (how the *Norton Anthology* table of contents has changed, how mimeographed copies of *Their Eyes Were Watching God* circulated at National Women's Studies Association conferences). This class is enriched by the personal narratives they bring into it, by nonstandard language and idioms they know (and I don't). In other words, the traditional (solitary, disposable) assignment is inconsistent with the goals of the class. I wanted to develop a project that would both validate what students have to share – that is, to recognize their authority – and to approximate the public exchange of the classroom instead of losing a valuable resource when I hand back an essay only I have read.

The assignment I created asked students to contribute to a web resource offering various kinds of context for individual course readings. Instead of one long thesis-driven analytical argument, they produced five short points of connection with a text we'd read together, and instead of collecting papers in class, I set up a google site that would allow us to share what they produced with future students. The next cohort of Multicultural Lit students will be able to both access and add to this set of contributions, essentially collaborating with peers they've never been in the room with. In introducing the project to them, I was trying to situate both the value of reading and the project itself in a public framework (on the logic that reading together can be something more than parallel independent reading). To quote my assignment directly:

> As we've said, the kind of reading we do here is a communal practice: we come together to discuss what we're reading because we each bring a unique perspective, or background, or expertise to the room. And we need to bring something of the outside world into our classroom, because these texts speak from and to real-world experience. (For example: to understand power dynamics in a story, we need to think about the real social forces being represented in fiction; the more we investigate power dynamics in stories, the better we understand the operation of power in the real world.)

With this bidirectional flow of meaning in mind, I asked them to choose from among six types of contextual artifacts inviting varying degrees of personal connection. Again, quoting my assignment:

> **A footnote**: a word or cultural or historical reference that needs explanation. Your explanation may be researched in the conventional way, or you may be bringing your personal expertise to bear. (For example, you may know the nuances of a slang word, or you might know something of a particular cultural practice from your own family traditions.) In addition to the information you include, explain why it's important to know – i.e., how it helps readers understand the text.

With this category, I hoped to show students that their backgrounds count as expertise – that they bring something worth knowing to the classroom. At the same time, I wanted to give them the agency to ask and answer their own questions, to ask themselves what they're curious about.

> **In the news**: make a connection between your text and a current event (either current to us or contemporary with the text's publication). (For example, when we read Silko's "Lullaby," we'll draw a parallel to a current adoption case that echoes some of the story's conflicts.) This piece should include a careful summary of the event plus a thoughtful justification for including it as context for this text.

Here, we reinforce the idea that fiction is a reworking of the real world, not an escape from it.

> **Theoretical context**: for example, you might find that a concept from your sociology or psychology or political science or anthropology (etc.)

class helps to illuminate what's going on in the text. Again, summarize carefully and explain what exactly the concept helps us see in the text.

Students have been taught to see general education requirements as classes to "get out of the way" so they can concentrate on the major; I would like them to experience these required courses as part of a coherent education.

> **Image**: what would you put on the cover of this book (or story or poem) and why? What interpretation of the text does the image suggest? (Although you should describe it in your own words, be sure to include the image with your explanation of how it works with the text.)

It's interesting to me how the triangulation of analysis – engaging with a text by way of an independent image – often allows students to more fully express an interpretation.

> **About the author**: what biographical background information would really help readers make sense of the text? Your information should be precise and purposeful: birthplace and odd jobs held and other books written may or may not offer a key to the text, but something like Junot Diaz's narrative of sexual assault surely does. Integrate your explanation of relevance into the material you include here.

The idea here was to make the writer a person for them – a person about whom they might have some curiosity.

> **Personal narrative**: Your life experiences certainly influence how you understand a text. Tell your story and then explain its connection to the story or poem you're working on. (And just remember that this resource will be shared with future readers, so only disclose what you're comfortable making public.)

Storytelling of this kind gets a bad rap, as an alternative to rather than a source of textual analysis. It is certainly true that solipsistic self-regard can prevent students from engaging with the text, but I hoped here to develop rather than stifle the instinct.

As noted in the descriptions, we modeled some of these categories in class. For example, after reading some stories from Junot Diaz's *Drown*, we read his agonizing *New Yorker* essay breaking the silence around being raped as a child. Not that autobiography provides the answer key, of course; but this dimension added some nuance to our discussion of gender dynamics in the stories. In the essay, Diaz offers a re-reading of his own behaviors, his disengagement and cruelty and wearing of masks, through the lens of his trauma, a perspective that allows masks and trauma and masculinity in the stories to take on additional layers of meaning. (I'll note that the precision of this example was difficult to replicate, though; biographical context they produced for the assignment was often just the Wikipedia overview, so I would say this connection needs more attention to make it work in the future.)

I also assigned a chapter from a social psychology textbook on multicultural competence in order to make the point that the study of literature is intrinsically interdisciplinary, that what they're learning in other classes enriches their readings. By highlighting this kind of connection, I hoped to encourage them to be more conscious of relationships between classes, to deepen their learning in Sociology or Biology or Psychology by applying it here. But this also gave us an occasion to talk more about what reading can make happen. The class is mostly set up like the goal is understanding the text, but the goal of understanding the text is presumably acting in the world with awareness and intention. Not adopting an ideology, I hope, but maybe adopting an orientation.

In a similar way, a contemporary news story helped students connect with Leslie Marmon Silko's "Lullaby," from her 1981 collection *Storyteller*. Students found the story, in which a Navajo mother's children are taken away by government agents – "for their own good," of course – a little obscure. I nudged them with some material on Grandmother Spider because this was what had opened the story up for me years ago, but trying to illuminate a history they didn't know (Indigenous land and culture loss resulting from Anglo policies) with a cultural tradition they didn't know (Grandmother Spider and the creative power of storytelling) served to confound their confusion. However, Jan Hoffman's "Who Can Adopt a Native Child? A Texas Couple vs. 573 Tribes" made some of the story's issues a little more immediately available for them. The case detailed in this *New York Times* story revolves around a child whose birth parents are Navajo and Cherokee and the white couple that wants to adopt him; they are blocked by the Indian Child Welfare Act, which gives priority to Native families in adoption cases. Students could see a lot of the dynamics of the story replayed in this case, even in the photos accompanying the article – which in turn allowed them to engage with the story. This context was very helpful for making the point that what we're reading about is happening around us, even now – that we read stories as a way of participating more deeply in the real world, and not as a way of satisfying gen ed requirements.

Although I presented the class with these models, one goal was to shift some research from me to them – to see what they thought needed contextualizing or explaining, what connections they would make, instead of doing all the deciding (and collecting) myself. This assignment required some difficult analytical moves – choosing an appropriate artifact or approach, figuring out what needs to be explained, and articulating its significance for our understanding of the novel – but I hoped to put them in a more active role, so they weren't passively articulating a prescribed contextual connection. However, since what for some students might be "funds of knowledge" are for others just research questions, this poses some challenges. As Laurie Grobman writes in "Toward a Multicultural Pedagogy," multicultural scholars agree about the value of decentering the classroom, shifting power and agency from teacher to learner, but putting this goal into practice is not so simple. How much control over the class (and the syllabus) should instructors relinquish? Is there a point at which it's irresponsible, leads to a misuse of class materials? Is it disingenuous to suggest that a classroom can be decentered, given the weight of teacher's opinion? "How do we reconcile [Michael J.] Savage's claim [in "Authors, Authority, and the Graduate Student Teacher: Against Canonical Pedagogy"] that classroom discussion is successful only to the extent that we 'find ways to empower students to set the agenda, to lead the class toward their own interests' with the necessity for contextual knowledge in the reading of multicultural literatures?" (227). There's a delicate balance here: the instructor may not want to assert authority, but they do need to bring expertise. In other words, I want to authorize student-driven readings, but without cultural knowledge as a corrective, students writing about cultural identities not their own might default to universalizing on the one hand or to othering on the other. By asking for both personal narrative and research, I'm hoping to, in some sense, have it both ways: to foreground the need for context, but make students responsible for developing that context, so that they will perhaps listen more carefully for where a footnote is needed or where a connection is possible (and in so doing, develop their cultural competence).

Although I could immediately see some areas for improvement, as I'll discuss below, some good things came out of this assignment. For example, a student I'll call Maya, who almost never voluntarily participated in discussion, wrote about *The Joy Luck Club* in ways that demonstrate a lot of what I'd hoped to accomplish. Her personal narrative focused on her identification, as a child of one Asian parent, with biracial Lena St. Clair. Maya wrote about living up to Asian stereotypes, about her discomfort traveling to meet her family in the Philippines and being seen as lower class for her sun-darkened skin. I'd had her in class before, but had never heard about this aspect of her identity. I also appreciated that she drew a connection to Trump administration immigration policy for her "in the news" entry. Some students insist that the course conform to their melting pot mentality; they want the Ellis Island narrative, want to enjoy cultural difference without addressing discrimination. (I remember how stunned I was some years ago when a student issued a complaint that the course was "too political." What, I had naively wondered, did she expect?) For this Asian student from California, the encounter with an immigrant story triggered a very different frame of reference. Perhaps for this reason, Maya seemed to engage with this assignment in a way she hadn't with more traditional essays. As an index of her interest, she put the time and effort into drawing an image for her cover instead of just finding something online. The drawing itself was impressive, but

I was even more struck by the way she used it to articulate her reading of the novel, using shadows and silhouettes, as she explained in her accompanying statement, to illustrate cultural and familial influences. This alternate analytical path unlocked some ideas that might not have come out in a more traditional format.

It was students like Maya for whom this assignment was most successful – students whose stories tended not to make it into the room. I am reminded here of one important lesson from our covid year: Zoom class, in my experience, was disastrous except for the explosion of commentary from some students in the chat. Although by reflex I equate verbal participation with commitment to the discussion, that's because these are academic conventions I've internalized and feel comfortable with myself. When Zoom chat gave students an alternative to putting up a hand, I was reminded that a gesture I find effortless may be fraught with anxiety for some students. The barriers to entry are far lower in the chat, when one doesn't need to capture the attention of the room, or find out in real time that a thought isn't fully baked after all. Some students are extremely forthcoming with personal narrative in class discussion; for other students who want to share their stories and ideas but don't want a spotlight during class, this kind of assignment offers another route.

Another quiet student whom I'll call Reina also produced interesting work. Her response to the assignment showed the value of moving in two directions, balancing personal reflection with research. Although white and from a conservative family, she was able to find a way into Rahul Mehta's "Quarantine" by identifying with the protagonist as a queer person, but she resisted the temptation to let that identification override cultural difference. In contextualizing the story, she connected with what she did know but also looked up something she didn't (the Hare Krishna commune to which the protagonist takes his grandfather). What I appreciated even more was her insight into the multicultural reading process: as she wrote, "you learn to care more about a story when you understand the information and culture. When you don't know a character's culture, you can skim or forget certain things because you don't get it immediately so you don't feel like it's worth getting." What she's describing doesn't sound like gratuitous research for an assignment as much as awareness of the way relationships are made.

I would also add that this assignment seemed to make some space for a different kind of conversation during office hours. There was one student I'd never been able to connect with who came for the first time to my office to discuss this project. In the course of our conversation, I heard a lot more about where he was from and what he cared about, and he also wrote much more directly about racism here than in other assignments. This suggests to me that there's value simply in announcing that I'm interested enough in their stories to make them part of the formal work of the course. I take for granted that this is obvious to them from the tenor of our class discussions and the way I've set up the class, but I think I underestimate the preconceptions some students have about what professors are. I often hear students articulate their surprise that professors actually seem to care about them, because they'd been told to expect scholarly distance. Building this kind of personal inquiry into the course may help those students to take seriously that I think they matter.

Gains like these, of course, could be had from a disposable assignment that simply defined the writing task in a less conventional way. And that, because of some mistakes on my part, is pretty much how most students experienced this project. I heard them describe it as a "ten page paper," because that's what it was for them: a ten-page paper in five parts. One important learning experience here was how thoroughly we've all been institutionalized – both students and professors needed more cues to really rethink what we were doing.

One reason they still felt like they were just writing something for the teacher was because they were: it was due at the very end of the semester, because I was thinking as I always have, and big projects are due at the end. This means they had no opportunity (unless they were curious enough to look after the class was over) to see that they were writing in public.

I told them their work was for future readers, but those readers remained pretty abstract; they had no real awareness of an audience, and because what they turned in was still just a Word document (since I uploaded content to our site myself), it just seemed like business as usual. There's a missed opportunity in terms of motivation, since for one thing, students will likely put more care and effort into a piece their peers will see. In addition, I think there's something to be said for the more luxurious feel of the online format. A Word document is made to be discarded, but a web page, even with the minimal sophistication of a google site template, seems like more of an occasion. (A colleague of mine has students contribute blog posts for his film studies class, and I'm always struck by the writing quality; I think both writer and reader react to the visual appeal of the platform.) So by failing to foreground the audience or the medium, I reinforced the teacher-student dyad and all the lack of investment it enables.

The grading rubric was part of the problem too. It looks just like the rubric for any other essay – it rewards clarity and precision, skilled use of textual evidence, depth of understanding. These are good things to reward, but it means I left the fundamental structure of the traditional assignment – the academic discourse that alienates – in place. I know why I did that; it's the old assessment problem again. The qualities that I may value or want to encourage (authentic engagement, for example) feel harder to measure, or harder to make transparent. So I found myself rewarding institutional fluency, with some begrudging As on articulate, carefully cited, relatively lifeless work. The most revealing case is the student who, writing about *Behold the Dreamers*, Imbolo Mbue's novel about Cameroonian immigrants, doesn't even mention that she herself is from Africa until deep into the project. She is extremely good at school, and I didn't persuasively ask her to be something else. In short, as long as I continue to think of this in terms of the traditional assignment, or at least in terms of traditional timelines and rubrics, there's no reason why it would feel more authentic to them. It's just another set of rules to follow. When I revise this rubric for future use, I'll be more mindful of the fact that a rubric is a statement of values as much as it is a grading tool.

I will also build in some of the brainstorming and feedback processes I neglected in this first iteration. In addition to short-circuiting the revision process with my ill-considered timeline, I missed some opportunities to help students develop more thoughtful responses through more frequent reflective writing. This will be a more valuable resource for future students if I focus a little less on *information* as context, make it a little less of a research project. I think it's important to maintain the idea of informed reading to guard against facile universalization or cultural incompetence, so I don't mean to abandon citation altogether; but questions can be just as useful as answers in working toward an understanding of a text. A student who is able to articulate what they don't know can open up a productive line of inquiry.

And as this last point suggests, the more fundamental potential for this as a collaboration can be developed when future students enter into the already populated rooms of this web resource. I will ask students to take an active role in curating the site, identifying less useful contributions for removal, but they'll also have opportunities to build on existing content. For example, one entry for *Their Eyes Were Watching God* draws a parallel between the 1928 hurricane that flooded Lake Okeechobee and the similarly destructive Hurricane Katrina; an incoming student who wanted to explore racial dynamics in the aftermath of both disasters would have much to elaborate on. Likewise, a Latinx student might want to enter into dialogue with the personal narrative in an existing entry for *The House on Mango Street* in which a Latina student describes her view of Hispanic attitudes toward education.

Reflecting on the goals of this assignment, I am reminded that success with NDAs hinges on accurately assessing what students can contribute. The NDA loses value if what they do is something I could always do better. Wiley et al assert, "Having witnessed an existence proof of the creation of excellent novice-produced content in the Wikipedia context, there is reason to believe it may be possible that novices (students) might be able to produce excellent open content in educational settings as well" (Wiley et al 62). But while Wikipedia is created on an amateur basis, it isn't made exclusively by novices (I can only imagine what a whole Wikipedia written by first-year students would be like). Students do have their own forms of expertise, however; they can provide perspectives and contexts that have nothing to do with professional credentials. So for this assignment to succeed, I need to be clear about the kinds of expertise they can provide and what a community of readers can do.

This is an opportunity to consider some fundamental questions about the literature classroom. Am I requiring attendance as discipline for discipline's sake, or because there really is something that happens in the room? Is what's happening in the room something *I'm* doing, or something *we're* doing? Bruns makes the point that writing about the teaching of literature tends to focus on the actions of the teachers, not the students; we may see ourselves as student-centered, but our classroom practice doesn't necessarily live up to those ideals. Quoting a typical entry from MLA's *Approaches to Teaching* series, a description of how the text would be explicated, she asks, "how does an analysis such as this, with no reference to students or teachers or any speakers at all, illustrate a class discussion?" (82). Significantly, the instructor quoted references his "discussion" of a point. I use the word this way too – "discussion" for something like "exploration." But one is supposed to be about exchange; the explorer may be solitary, but a discussion is different. Defining what a student-centered assignment is asking for and developing the potential for NDAs means determining what a discussion (as opposed to a punctuated lecture) is made of.

One thing I know they have that I don't is a student's perspective, and so I can see real value in NDAs with a teaching focus (i.e., projects oriented toward future students). This is the logic behind another experiment I'll briefly describe, this one in an interdisciplinary Intro to Social Justice Studies class. Over the course of a few semesters, I'd observed an increasingly dramatic bifurcation of test grades: students who were good at tests got As, while some students who were far more valuable to class discussion struggled to pass. A grade distribution that so clearly reflected educational privilege was particularly galling given the class content, so I replaced two major tests with video presentations asking students to choose a key concept (like the social construction of race, or confirmation bias, or the representativeness heuristic, or privilege) and explain it to future learners. I did this because being able to define a concept on a test isn't as important as being able to use it to explain something in the world. I will probably always be better at the textbook definition, but their explanations and applications may certainly be more useful than mine, particularly when communicating with peers.

The video presentation for future students is certainly a project I'll incorporate into other classes; it did serve my primary goal of neutralizing the advantage of institutional skills, and it was surely a more meaningful exercise than passive memorization of terms. For this to work as well as it could, though, a little more scaffolding would be helpful. Some students struggled to make their own connections; when asked to describe the operation of the concept in their own experience, they googled for examples rather than thinking it through for themselves. This isn't so surprising, since I'd only ever demonstrated the endpoint, not the process; I gave them real-world examples but left my mental steps opaque, which is like showing the answers but not how to get them. Next time around, we'll develop some questions to work through (and we'll make use of a more structured drafting and revision process as well).

Ultimately, my purpose in describing these experiments is to gesture toward a mindset shift, a rethinking of what assignments are for. So far, I've broken a traditional assignment into some smaller, differently shaped pieces and tried to open up the classroom walls by putting it online where future learners can participate in its creation, and I've replaced a test that does nothing but earn points with a peer education resource. I can imagine trying to create more connections with the real world that further destabilize traditional forms. For example, we have lots of unused exhibit space in our hallways and classroom walls; we could serve a few different purposes with, for example, a poster series that would both give our readings a public function and, depending on the content of our posters, perhaps reshape the institutional environment to send a different message about who belongs there. (A visual space audit could be an interesting first step for that project: whose faces and whose words are in our public places?) Or I could have students respond to the text in the form of a letter to a real person that would actually be sent (*Dear X, I think you should read this book and here's why*, or *this poem made me think of you and here's how*). If I'm going to keep making the spirited argument that literature matters, it will help to stop throwing so much work away. I am invigorated by the possibility of forging more connections between the work of the class and the reasons I think we're there in the first place.

Bibliography

Acevedo, Elizabeth. "I use my poetry to confront violence against women." TEDxMidatlantic Salon: Everyone Values Equality. https://www.youtube.com/watch?v=SJ0G1iCLzCA. Accessed 7 June 2021.

Alexander, Jonathan and Jacqueline Rhodes. "Flattening Effects: Composition's Multicultural Imperative and the Problem of Narrative Coherence." *College Composition and Communication*, vol. 65, no. 3, February 2014, pp. 430-454. https://www.jstor.org/stable/43491483

Bruns, Cristina Vischer. *Why Literature? The Value of Literary Reading and What It Means for Teaching*. NY, Continuum, 2011.

Corrigan, Paul T. "The State of Scholarship on Teaching Literature." *Pedagogy*, vol. 18, no. 3, October 2018, pp. 415-32.

Diaz, Junot. "The Silence: The Legacy of Childhood Trauma." *The New Yorker*, 9 April 2018, https://www.newyorker.com/magazine/2018/04/16/the-silence-the-legacy-of-childhood-trauma. Accessed 7 June 2021.

Grobman, Laurie. "Toward a Multicultural Pedagogy: Literary and Nonliterary Traditions." *MELUS*, vol. 26, no. 1, Spring 2001, pp. 221-240.

Hoffman, Jan. "Who Can Adopt a Native Child? A Texas Couple vs. 573 Tribes." *New York Times*, 5 June 2019. https://www.nytimes.com/2019/06/05/health/navajo-children-custody-fight.html. Accessed 7 June 2021.

Linkon, Sherry Lee. *Literary Learning: Teaching the English Major*. Indiana UP, 2011.

Mehta, Rahul. "Quarantine." *New Stories from the South: The Year's Best, 2009*. Ed. Madison Smartt Bell. Chapel Hill, NC, Algonquin, 2009, pp. 191-207.

Rodriguez, Richard. "Aria." *Growing Up Latino: Memoirs and Stories*. Ed. Harold Augenbraum and Ilan Stavans. Houghton Mifflin, 1993, pp. 305-328.

Seraphin, Sally B., J. Alex Grizzell, Anastasia Kerr-German, Marjorie A. Perkins, Patrick R. Grzanka, and Erin Hardin. "A Conceptual Framework for Non-Disposable Assignments: Inspiring Implementation, Innovation, and Research." *Psychology Learning and Teaching*, vol. 18, no. 1, Mar. 2019, pp. 84–97. http://dx.doi.org.ezproxy.snhu.edu/10.1177/1475725718811711

Verschelden, Cia. *Bandwidth Recovery: Helping Students Reclaim Cognitive Resources Lost to Poverty, Racism, and Social Marginalization*. Sterling, VA, Stylus Publishing, 2017.

White, John Wesley and Patrick R. Lowenthal. "Minority College Students and Tacit 'Codes of Power': Developing Academic Discourses and Identities." *The Review of Higher Education*, vol. 34, no. 2, Winter 2011, pp. 283-318.

Wiley, David. "What is Open Pedagogy?" *Iterating Toward Openness: Open Content*. OpenContent.org. 21 Oct 2013. https://opencontent.org/blog/archives/2975

Wiley, David et al. "A Preliminary Exploration of the Relationships Between Student-Created OER, Sustainability, and Students' Success." *International Review of Research in Open and Distributed Learning*, vol. 18, no. 4, June 2017, pp. 60-69.

Chapter 5
Renewable Assignments, from Paper to Trees

Allison M. Cummings
Southern New Hampshire University

Abstract

Allison Cummings (Southern New Hampshire University) considers the topic of nondisposable assignments from the perspective of renewable (human) resources in "Renewable assignments, from paper to trees." Mapping tools have inspired a range of innovative projects for building ecological literacy; her survey of the field, grounded in pedagogical scholarship around what makes assignments meaningful, describes projects in the Environmental Humanities that foster "an ethic of connection to community or planet." Her digital Nature Log assignment, for example, pins student contributions to google maps, resulting in a public multimedia story of place; similarly, a video project gives students an opportunity to "read" landscape in a way that generates questions about land use. But at the same time, Cummings is realistic in her view of what such public-facing assignments actually do, and she offers a moving defense of private writing that creators – like her own great grandmother – could have disposed of but chose not to.

Keywords: Environmental Humanities, environmental literature, educational technology, story mapping, open pedagogy

***

This paper will consider "renewable assignments" for literature classes that aim to create environmental knowledge, awareness, and ethics among the students who write them, along with practicing the usual skills of critical analysis and writing. The notion of "renewable" in this context, then, draws not only from recent ideas for engaging assignments, but from the household understanding of environmentally renewable resources. In the pages that follow, I'll begin with a brief, introductory tour of some of the research focused on renewable assignments and similarly meaningful assignments, argue for the value of traditional, private writing alongside writing for wider audiences, and then detail the specific renewable assignments this essay promises. Since this article began as a paper delivered just days before the pandemic shutdown of March 2020 and has been written while teaching remote classes, I will briefly add consideration of how these assignments might be shaped by online teaching and learning.

Scanning the Field

I am not a specialist in open pedagogy, rhetoric and composition, education, the digital humanities, or the environmental humanities, so my scan of the literature pertaining to renewable assignments will certainly be introductory and partial. However, I include a brief overview both to provide some context for others new to the discourse and to situate my pedagogy amid the frames that have shaped it.

First, the terms "disposable," "non-disposable assignments" (NDAs), "renewable," "high-impact," and "meaningful assignments" are all kissing cousins, but there are some distinctions between them, delineated below. In their conference call for papers on this topic, Alfred University professors Melissa Ryan and Kerry Kautzman quoted David Wiley's characterization of "disposable assignments." In a 2013 post on his Open Content blog, called "What is Open Pedagogy," Wiley calls for "killing the disposable assignment," proclaiming that these assignments "add no value to the world – after a student spends three hours creating it, a teacher spends 30 minutes grading it, and then the student throws it away. Not only do these assignments add no value to the world; they actually suck value out of the world." David Wiley has been actively aiming to make educational content open and accessible to all since 1998, has been an early and prolific advocate of open-educational resources (OER), including textbooks, and helped spur the now massive Creative Commons site/movement about twenty years ago.

While good teachers have always tried to offer their students engaging writing assignments, since around 2000, many of those efforts have been shaped by the internet and other user-friendly technologies. OER texts, for example, depend upon the web, and ideally, on faculty who are able to offer the same course over several years and on motivated students with dependable writing skills. For open pedagogy advocates like Wiley, worthwhile assignments take place on the web and contribute to public knowledge through it. Moreover, as University of British Columbia professor Christina Hendricks observes on a teaching blog, Wiley regards renewable assignments as useful insofar as they can be revised or repurposed by future users: "In order to be 'renewable,' student work needs to have an open license: a license that explicitly states that others may revise and reuse the material without asking for permission from the copyright holder" (Hendricks). Clearly not all student or scholarly work should be open to revision, as James Skidmore explores in this volume. The term "renewable" serves also to advocate not only for assignments useful to future students or the wider world, but for transforming time spent learning into time spent producing. "Open education *resources*" (italics mine) treat the student time spent producing knowledge and the faculty time spent evaluating knowledge as (human) resources, to be wisely managed. Since open-education texts also aim to be free of charge, they also aim to save financial resources.

One key feature of "non-disposable assignments" that answer Wiley's call, then, is their public-facing, utilitarian aims. In "A Conceptual Framework for Non-Disposable Assignments: Inspiring Implementation, Innovation, and Research," Sally Seraphin, along with five colleagues from the University of Tennessee -Knoxville, offers a comprehensive literature review of recent scholarship on "non-disposable assignments" (NDAs) and observes, in a list of Five Principles of NDAs, "we have trouble envisioning how a good NDA would be produced in isolation" (86). After their overview of the field, Seraphin at al. define the major components of non-disposable assignments and propose that assignments gain value in proportion to their impacts across time (i.e., beyond the course), across space (beyond the classroom, institution, or community), and through gravity ("impact on learning, per defined objectives" (90), by the student or others). They encourage future researchers to build on their time-space-gravity framework and further assess NDAs' value "for students and humankind."

Seraphin et al. also trace the origins of the field to open-education advocacy, giving ample kudos to David Wiley and others, writing that discussion of "the concept of NDAs, including those referred to as 'renewable assignments,' has grown in popularity in . . . select education circles, alongside an enthusiastic push toward open pedagogy" (84). The keywords included in their abstract help situate renewable assignments as close kin to "NDAs, service learning, experiential learning, open-educational resources (OER), open pedagogy" (84). Their extensive bibliography includes papers from across fields, but most heavily represents journals in the fields of Education, Psychology, Media, and Human Resources, in that order. It's worth noting that none of their sources come from journals in English or Rhetoric-composition or specifically focus on writing. So, while the article is full of ideas applicable to literature and writing courses, single-authored writing assignments are not its primary aim.[1] Nevertheless,

---

[1] Collaborative writing assignments can certainly help build student community as they incorporate "low-stakes" practice runs of assignments. Less-proficient writing students can see models of clearer organization and writing from peers with stronger skills. However, sometimes weaker students use collaborative writing assignments as a free ride

many faculty who teach writing or work in the Digital Humanities can and do incorporate the kinds of collaborative, peer-reviewed, community-oriented writing assignments Seraphin et al. describe, such as course-created websites, open-access textbooks, digitized archival projects, infographics, informational videos, or websites that can be shared with community partners in service learning courses or with the wider world—along with traditional, individually-authored writing.

The technologies in Digital Humanities or just tech-savvy literature courses may include platforms like Hypothes.is, Social Book, Perusal, or Commentpress. Starting in spring 2021, my Nature Writers class will sign into *The Reader's Thoreau*, an existing online annotation platform that allows teachers to put students in reading groups and "showcase their conversations or keep them private" (*Reader's Thoreau*). Students can post their questions and interpretations on the text, line by line, and read others' annotations as well, including those of Thoreau scholars. Even if a professor keeps the class's annotations private, students are likely to feel their contributions are part of a larger scholarly conversation, since they can see their classmates' thoughts and potentially thousands of others' posts on the text as well.

Like the Digital Humanities, and often integrating technology into courses, the Environmental Humanities encompasses courses in literature, writing, film, history, and other courses in the Humanities that focus on environmental issues. A wonderful collection of syllabi and teaching resources for courses that include environmental themes is available on the Teaching Resources Database for the Association for the Study of Literature and the Environment (ASLE). Within the Environmental Humanities, literature and writing courses focused on the environment have long included assignments that are renewable in various ways, though not necessarily in Wiley's ways. A common foundational assignment in eco-composition courses focuses on place;[2] in recent years, many courses that include a focus on place have made use of online mapping tools. For instance, students at all levels may drop pins on a collaborative class map and record specific features of the landscape or weather or write poems or descriptions on a place. Such records can easily serve public knowledge, contributing local observations to citizen-science programs like the Great Backyard Bird Count, FrogWatch USA and others.

---

to a higher grade. Thus the individual writing assignment still seems a necessary exercise to get developing writers and less motivated students to actually practice writing and display what needs work.

[2] See Sidney Dobrin, *Saving Place: An Ecocomposition Reader*, 2005, which supports courses focused on place.

Two especially valuable course projects on place are Elizabeth Rush's "community-engaged" 2016 Digital Humanities course at Bates College in Maine and William Cronon's courses for graduate and undergraduate students at the University of Wisconsin-Madison. Neither of these projects took place in literature courses, but I will explore below how each could be adapted for literature courses specifically. In a brief stint teaching at Bates, Rush asked her students to interview people who work on the land in Maine about how climate change, or "the weather," is affecting their lives and livelihoods.[3] Students interviewed "a beekeeper, a raspberry farmer, a member of the Stanton Bird Club, a Wabanaki historian, a forester, and a bait shop owner" (Rush, "Climate") and incorporated the responses into brief essays, along with photos, videos, and podcasts that they assembled on a "story map" of climate change in Maine ("Climate Change in Maine"). In an essay she published about the project, "Climate Change and the Stories We Tell," Rush details why and how she conducted this assignment. She notes that the students' sense of a larger audience, of the urgency of climate action, and of ethical responsibility to represent their interviewees' stories accurately all made the project meaningful: "In the end, it was precisely the *public* nature of the digital project—both its easily searchable URL and the end of the semester launch event—that gave meaning to the work students produced" (Rush, italics mine). For anyone contemplating a similarly community-engaged, project-based course, Rush's essay is essential reading; and for faculty without the time, institutional support, or technological skill to undertake quite such an ambitious endeavor, Rush helpfully points out how one might adjust this project to accommodate constraints of time, money, or tech expertise. The course and resulting map site are stellar examples of a non-disposable assignment of great public value that is also profoundly meaningful to students and develops multiple skills at once.

Another example of student work that contributes to public understanding of place and the environment comes from Professor William Cronon's courses at the University of Wisconsin-Madison. Cronon has assembled WordPress sites at williamcronon.net that encompass his courses, scholarship, civic contributions to his community, and resources in the field of Environmental History. One particular gem exists at the site, "Forest Hill Cemetery: A Guide: A Romantic Landscape in Madison, Wisconsin." Cronon guided a small seminar of graduate students to research and collaboratively create a beautiful virtual guidebook to the cultural and environmental history of a local historic cemetery (Forest Hill). With sections on "Effigy Mounds," the "Geography of

---

[3] Rush went on to write *Rising: Dispatches from the New American Shore*, a non-fiction Pulitzer nominee that includes extensive interviews with people displaced by sea-level rise.

Death," and "A Body's Journey," along with guides to the historic headstones and history of the cemetery, this project not only broadens a (real or virtual) visitor's understanding of that place but contributes to cultural understandings of the rituals and concepts of death and the afterlife over eons.

Of course, numerous teachers at every level have generously posted similarly helpful examples of their courses, assignments, and specialties; and those sites, particularly where they include student writing that can serve as models for students worldwide, certainly offer examples of renewable assignments, projects that are authentically worthwhile for future students and that contribute knowledge or value to the wider world. I point out these two because they are specifically focused on place and on the intersections of nature and culture in those places. Though neither took place in literature courses, it isn't hard to extrapolate from these models. For example, a course that includes regional writing might invite students to analyze and compare literary representations to historical, geographical, or scientific representations of that particular place or landscape and post the comparisons on a website, or create a video of a particular landscape's changes over time for use in classrooms, state historical archives, or planning board meetings.

A number of pedagogical scholars, particularly writing specialists, have explored what makes writing projects meaningful and memorable to students, whether that writing contributes to public knowledge or not. There are two large-scale, multi-year studies that I will mention here because they are especially applicable for renewable assignments in literature courses, though neither use the term "renewable" or the rhetoric of public-facing, revisable open pedagogy. One project is Paul Anderson, Chris Anson, Robert Gonyea, and Charles Paine's writing based on National Study of Student Engagement (NSSE) data from 72,000 students on "high-impact writing assignments."[4] Anderson et al. have presented their findings in several articles between 2015 and 2017, with different emphases for audiences of faculty, writing-across-the-curriculum directors, or administrators. Another ongoing study is Michele Eodice, Anne Ellen Geller, and Neal Lerner's "meaningful writing project" begun in 2012 and still collecting information in 2019, which likewise appears in multiple formats. Both projects testify to the value of private writing for

---

[4] Additional authors join Anderson, Anson, Gonyea, and Price on "How Writing Contributes to Learning," the short presentation of their research. These authors are Tom Fish, Margaret Marshall, Wendy Menefee-Libey, Laura Palucki Blake, and Susan Weaver, from a range of institutions.

students' learning and development, and offer specific, practical advice for crafting engaging writing assignments in any field.

While all of Anderson et al.'s findings can't fit in a paragraph, here are a few key points. Students find writing assignments most engaging when 1) they have the opportunity to talk with others about the ideas and draft, including peers, family, classmates, and faculty, before the writing is due[5] (which the authors refer to as "Interactive Writing Processes"); 2) they must think critically or creatively or synthesize multiple texts or sources of information ("Meaning-Making Writing Tasks"); and 3) they have clear instructions on both the assignment (including directions, examples) and how they will be evaluated ("Clear Writing Expectations") (Anderson, et al. "How Writing" 5-6). Additionally, underlying or preceding these tasks, students learn best when they trust the teacher, trust other students in the class, feel that the subject matter and class discussion are inclusive of different identities and backgrounds, when they are interested in the subject matter, are able to connect that subject matter to other courses or their own experiences, when they reflect on their own work, and when they feel the assignment contributes to "personal and social development" ("How to Create" 10).

The last finding to highlight from Anderson et al. will be the most cherished and perhaps new to faculty who assign substantial amounts of writing. The researchers italicize it for emphasis: "*the three constructs developed in this study had much higher correlations with engagement in deep learning than did the amount of writing*" (6). "The constructs" refer to the frames quoted in parenthesis above: "interactive writing processes" and so on. Anderson et al. are directing their remarks largely to faculty and administrators who are working to improve student writing through writing across the curriculum programs; so, for buy-in from faculty across disciplines, this finding is helpful indeed. For faculty in literature and writing courses, who spend their professional lives buried under (now virtual) stacks of papers, this suggests they may not need to assign any more or *even as much* writing as they presently do; rather, they should take care

---

[5] It's worth noting here that students found value in some form of sharing and discussing their ideas and writing *before* the assignment was due. Many faculty try to include peer review and respond to drafts before writing is due, and while we may focus on the students who don't submit drafts or who despise peer review, a significant percentage of the students NSSE surveyed apparently appreciated the chance to talk through and improve their ideas and writing-- when the process of peer review was well defined and modeled. Since the emphasis in renewable assignments is on sharing *after* the writing is done, one wonders if students value the sharing of their ideas at *any* stage, to have an audience and get more feedback on their ideas, or if the benefits of sharing differ at each stage in the process.

that the writing they *do* assign meets as many of the key criteria as possible to have the maximum impact on students' learning.

One necessary feature of, say, Rush's Climate Change in Maine map site or most course blogs is brevity: most shared, digital writing assignments, whether on a website, podcast, or video, require considerably shorter and less detailed text than a standard academic term paper of fifteen to twenty pages. Consequently, faculty may worry that students writing shorter texts in digital formats will not get the kind of immersive, meditative experience that yields lasting advances in critical thinking skills. Anderson et al.'s studies indicate that that worry may be unfounded. Though there are still undeniable benefits to long, immersive writing projects, Anderson's analysis of the data suggests that the benefits of well-designed short writing assignments can be comparable. Therefore, the generally shorter formats of renewable writing assignments may lose little or no educational value in the transition from "paper" to pixels.

In their 2016 book, *The Meaningful Writing Project: Learning, Teaching, and Writing in Higher Education*, Michele Eodice, Anne Ellen Geller, and Neal Lerner report on a four-year study, starting in 2012. Eodice et al. sent out over 10,000 surveys to college seniors in 2012 at a range of institutions and collected over 700 responses. The survey questioned students about the details of writing assignments they had found meaningful over their college careers. The authors organize the chapters of their book around the key components students repeatedly cited as meaningful: "engagement with instructors, peers, and the material" (4), a sense of agency, and a sense of connection to their personal pasts and imagined future selves. Though their sample size is considerably smaller than Anderson's and their focus more granular, these findings map closely to the NSSE data, with "engagement" resembling Anderson's "interactive processes" and "agency" resembling "meaning making." The book offers anyone who assigns writing a thorough exploration of the ingredients of meaningful writing projects that students will remember and learn from, though they note that, unfortunately, meaningful, memorable writing assignments were the exception rather than the rule for most students. The researchers also maintain a website (http://meaningfulwritingproject.net/) that invites students to continue to contribute to the study, so as the dataset expands, the findings may become even more fine-grained. Readers interested in a review of scholarship on meaningful student writing can find overviews in both Eodice et al.'s 2016 book and a follow-up paper they published in 2019, "The Power of Personal Connection for Undergraduate Student Writers" (Eodice et al. "The Power").

In the 2019 article, Eodice, Geller, and Lerner take a deeper dive on that third point on personal connection. They write: "Meaningful writing assignments allow students to make and extend personal connections to their experiences or history (individual/ internal factors), their social relationships (social/

external factors), and/or their subjects and topics for writing (a combination of individual and social factors)" (321). While students in their survey described some collaborative, renewable-type assignments, they also described more personal writing assignments that allowed room for creativity and personal growth. Nearly half (46% of student respondents) valued writing projects that allowed them to express themselves and their individual experiences and felt those allowed them to develop as writers and people (329). This observation connects nicely to the recommendation by numerous scholars of writing pedagogy to de-emphasize the conventions of academic writing, at least for some writing assignments, and instead allow and value the language of students' own discourse communities (324) for a more inclusive pedagogy (336) that engages and empowers students from all backgrounds. Along these lines, another key element of assignments that (16% of) students appreciated was the "opportunity to connect writing to peers, family, and community" (331). The Maine climate histories gathered in Elizabeth Rush's course could trace their impact on students partly to those elements of connection to family, community, and place.

While some of the writing assignments that students described for the Meaningful Writing Project study involved publicly shared work, many did not. Given this large-scale survey and the ongoing collection of students' own accounts of what they find meaningful, it seems hardly necessary to assert that students may still gain lasting benefits and skills through private writing assignments that are shared only with an instructor or class—particularly if those assignments allow students to find connections between the subject and their own lives, family, community, or their future goals. As this brief tour has perhaps also indicated, writing assignments may be "non-disposable" or "meaningful" (or disposable yet meaningful) regardless of whether they are publicly shared or solely private; what matters is that students see personal value and purpose in their work and learn skills and knowledge through that work. In contrast to Wiley's and others' skepticism about the value of private writings, I believe there can be great value in writing assignments that are not publicly shared, if they lead to self-discovery and growth or lay the groundwork for a larger ethic of connection to community or planet.

In the pages that follow, I will detail some of the writing assignments, both private and public-facing, that I've given my students in writing and literature courses, each of which aims to make students more aware of themselves and the natural world around them. Before we turn there, though, I will briefly digress to discuss some artifacts that illustrate my hesitation to declare only shared writing valuable.

Reading Tree Rings

I've saved and hauled around the country a large box of my high school and college papers, some handwritten, some typed. Maybe you have, too. I generally recall the *process* of writing them (alone, midnight to two, one draft), as well as what I wrote about, though generally not the grades. In a bureau drawer now, I also have a small sheaf of my grandmother's papers from her time at Mt. Holyoke College, including a handwritten gem dated Dec 6, 1918, titled, "Will the Airplane Ever be Commonly Used?" (teacher's comment: check), and a six-page study for Economics class, "Unemployment in the U.S. since the Armistice" dated May 1, 1919 (no grade or comment). She has several fictional stories, speculating about the "Farmerette" (female farm workers), a report on "The Slacker Raid in New York City," Sept 25, 1918, rounding up draft dodgers (the teacher's comment: "Good beginning and effective details. Conclusion impotent") and other creative and expository writings. WWI is woven into all my grandmother's college writings from 1918-19, but the Spanish flu gets no mention. Along with those papers, I have another small sheaf of *her* mother's school papers, my great-grandmother, Carrie Reed, including her 1886 Graduation Address to the senior class at West Boylston High School, Massachusetts, tied with a silk ribbon: "First of all, it seems of importance that we choose some work or profession..." There are several carefully folded poems and two small essays: one reevaluates the concept of "Trifles" and one, her least inspired, is called "Compositions."

First, there's the obvious point: my foremothers chose not to dispose of these assignments, tying them with ribbon and keeping them in drawers; and four unusually long generations of descendants chose not to dispose of them either. Did the writers ever reread these masterpieces? Yes, at least once, when they folded them together and chose to keep them. Did they ever think of what they wrote? I have no way to know that about my grandmother, though I recall her recounting the events of one essay: of going with classmates to sing for the "overseas men," now missing legs, arms, and eyes, in 1919. Now and then, I think of the twenty-page term paper I wrote in high school on the four paths to Buddhist enlightenment—though I got a C+. I could look back at the comment to learn what I did wrong (crummy citing? No argument?), but the grade doesn't matter now: only what I learned. Similarly, I vividly recall struggling to locate a central theme after close reading "The Wasteland" twenty-four times through, searching for handholds (pre-Internet. And we weren't supposed to consult critics). Were these writings meaningful? Well, my ancestors saved their creations for a reason, whether it was pride (it appears my great-grandmother was valedictorian) or a wish to preserve and look back at their younger selves. I doubt they were thinking of the future public uses of their ideas, although there are arguably some uses. They are meaningful to me now for reasons they could not have imagined: as family voices, windows into history, glimpses into the gendered experience of young women in 1886 and 1918, and now, artifacts of student writing from a century ago.

From these artifacts, I would argue that students need to find for themselves the personal meanings of an assignment, and in the process, generate motivation to think carefully about a subject or observe reality closely, as my grandmother watched a one-armed WWI vet begin to clap in time to the music with his buddy's nearby hand. The conclusions and connections students make in writing may help shape their thinking, their ethics, and their lives. Can that transformation be entirely or largely private? It seems so. And English writing classes are among the fields freest to offer students that latitude in their choice of subject, since subject matter is often secondary, if prescribed at all.

Circle-sailing

Each year my composition students, in a learning community with an Environmental Science course, write about a natural place they love, and reflect on how it has been a part of their growing up. The assignment's aim is to practice skills of description, narration, and research, and it lets me get to know where each student is "coming from" in both senses. In addition to describing the place in vivid imagery, students must find some research on the history of the built or natural environment and try to discern and describe traces of the past in the present landscape. The assignment borrows from William Cronon's Place Paper Assignment, and also from Sidney Dobrin's ideas about eco-composition and writing assignments on place. The premise of the exercise is that an awareness of place is the first step toward an attachment to natural places and a willingness to protect them. In "The Place, The Region, and the Commons," Gary Snyder suggests that a sense of the inter-connectedness of all life begins with love of a place: "the childhood landscape is learned on foot, and a map is inscribed in the mind. . . . to know the spirit of a place is to realize that you are a part of a part and that the whole is made of parts, each of which is whole. You start with the part you are whole in" (28, 41). In a writing course, an essay on place can serve the ends described above. In a literature course, it may serve additional ends.

I teach a 200-level, general-education Nature Writers course that attracts all majors and fulfills requirements for Environmental Science and English majors. In addition to incorporating canonical standards like Thoreau, Aldo Leopold, and Rachel Carson, I organize the course thematically and include recent environmental writing on race, gender, class, pollution/ environmental justice, animals, extinction, and climate change. Because it's a 200-level course for a general audience, there are not the same expectations for a twenty-page term paper, brimming with critical sources. As mentioned above, students will participate in the Digital Thoreau site; they'll also write weekly journals (some private, some public discussion posts on debated questions) that close read texts, and write a short, conventional literary analysis essay, which will also ask them to connect the text to their personal experience. Those assignments will fulfill the literature-specific course outcomes. Beyond those, I want students to spend some time off screens, outside, learning about species other than ours, and do some nature writing themselves.

This spring semester, the NatureWriters course, like all courses at my university, will be fully remote due to COVID-19. In an effort to create a sense of class community online, I'll create a course website and publish it online if the students consent. We'll begin by posting pins on a Google map for each student's town, though most students are in northern New England. To combat quarantine fatigue and build ecological literacy, I will ask students to go outside, look, listen, and record on their phones entries for a digital Nature Log that they'll post on the website. The posts can be photos, videos, sound files, drawings, and writings. Because it will be January, their first subject will be ice on a stream, river, or lake—or what should be ice, as even here in New Hampshire, winter now struggles to remain frozen. If we have snow, I'll ask them to find some tracks: deer, pigeon, chickadee, or squirrel, and identify whose feet made them. As the months elapse outside Zoom, they'll be able to track the first buds and insects. Downloading and using the i-Naturalist app on their phones, they can identify tree, plant, bird, and insect species, and write brief descriptions of the species, its location and status (endangered, threatened, invasive). If they choose to, they can share the observation to the iNaturalist site, which then feeds data points to a Global Biodiversity Information facility.[6] Any literature course that includes authors who kept detailed natural observations, such as Thoreau, Annie Dillard, Mary Oliver, Helen McDonald, might incorporate such a project, to allow students to blend the skills of close looking, research, and writing. The Nature Log is a renewable assignment insofar as the photos and species identifications can be useful for future students to compare to, and as mentioned, the posts could potentially be useful for citizen-science sorts of sites. The only literary components of the assignment, however, are the interpretive frames students bring from the course reading into their brief descriptions or commentaries.

In this course, I have also assigned a place essay, but one that incorporates literary texts. Students blend description, narration, historical research, interviews, literary textual connections, and reflection. Before these students write about place, they will have read multiple models of nature and environmental writing

---

[6] The iNaturalist site, a joint initiative of the California Academy of Sciences and the National Geographic Society, can be accessed at inaturalist.org.

and critiques of land use, from Thoreau's *Walden*, to Jewett's "A White Heron," to an excerpt from Jane Jacobs' *The Death and Life of Great American Cities*, to Juliana Spahr's poem, "Gentle Now, Don't Add to Heartache." They'll also read a few examples of eco-criticism to illuminate the literary texts and to model how they might approach writing about their own chosen place. That subject matter background clearly informs the personal and environmental reflections they produce: the last time I taught this course, one student cited Jacobs at length to explain how her recently rural town has sprawled and citified like so many other towns; another wove Thoreau through her meditations on how the Merrimack river runs through Manchester's history and her life; another conversed with Wendell Berry about how an ancestral farm had shrunken to a few acres with no animals or crops, reflecting widespread losses of small farms in New England. When I last taught the course, students shared these essays with peers before and after they were due, and many reported sharing the writing with their families. This spring, we can pin and link the place essays to the course map and site.

This assignment might therefore also qualify as renewable according to Wiley's ideas of open access, revisable contributions to public knowledge, and it would qualify as non-disposable because the map, Nature log posts, and place essays could be used as teaching tools for future iterations of the course. More importantly for these students, however, I would consider these projects "meaningful" and "high-impact" insofar as they foster critical analysis and research skills and allow students to connect the course material to their past experiences, their communities, and their diverse home identities. Most students reported they had never thought much about their geographical identities before, but through writing this piece, they now looked at the land around them in a new light. I hope their observations and understandings continue to deepen and be renewed as they move through the world.

Last time around, I offered a variant option for this assignment that would qualify as renewable, due to its intended public audience of future students and the campus and local communities. Instead of a paper, students had the option to create a collaborative video showing the transformation of a place over time: a "then and now" visual and textual portrait, incorporating historical images or maps, passages from literary texts, research on that place, and footage that the students would shoot. I had hoped students would "read" landscapes, as Claire Walker Leslie[7] or William Cronon describe, imagining what was there twenty,

---

[7] See Claire Walker Leslie and Charles E. Roth's *Nature Journaling*. VT: Storey Communications, 1998. In the chapter, "Nature Journaling with School Groups," Leslie recommends asking students to notice and try to "read" stone walls, glacial boulders, giant trees, old foundations or apple trees for clues to how nature and former inhabitants shaped the landscape.

fifty, one-hundred or four-hundred years before, discerning clues to past land use via giant trees, stone walls, glacial boulders, and so on, and then imagining future (ideal or dystopic) visions of what that site might look like in another fifty or 100 years, given present and future pressures on population, water, climate, and so on. I hoped they could illustrate these visions through a combination of photos, paintings, text, their own drawings and video, perhaps altering or creating images to illustrate the deep past and far future. To illustrate past and future, the students would need to do research in books, online, and in the archives of the college library and local Historical Societies and museums.

Just two students chose this option, making a video about the campus, which has changed drastically in the last fifteen years, expanding and erecting buildings at a furious pace. The campus has 338 acres; since 2010, the campus has cut down about half of the forests and shrubland, building at least eleven massive buildings and vast acres of parking. The rapid loss of forest and native plant life has now made the campus weirdly barren of birds or insects, though there is enough greenspace to support them. Since the student population rotates every four years, campus landscapes are especially subject to our amnesia about shifting (or declining) baselines. Having read about the concept of shifting baselines in class, I hoped the students could document how what we currently see, in terms of trees, plants, and wildlife, represents a loss of habitat and biodiversity even in the last twenty years.

I guess I envisioned a video showing time-lapse deforestation set to Wagnerian background music, a student-generated *Koyaanisqatsi* that would live on the school's website and compel administrators to run outside and call off the bulldozers, which were at that moment paving terraced parking lots in treeless asphalt steps down to the Merrimack. I hoped a video could give current students and staff a historical view of environmental degradation, for a visceral understanding of New Hampshire's recently rural but rapidly urbanizing environment. I imagined that future students or the surrounding community could then visualize and perhaps *create* a reforested or restored habitat, particularly as a buffer zone along the river. I wanted this assignment to change some minds, but as I'm suggesting, I had grandiose, dogmatic visions of what the students' project should be and accomplish—always a bad idea.

What the students created was more of a promotional video for the school. One student was a senior in Business-Marketing, pressed for time because he was already working full-time for BAE Systems, and the other was a senior Graphic Design major. They didn't manage to find time to use photos from the library archives, other than a few bird's-eye photos I had downloaded and sent them from the 1970s. They didn't get to the Historical Society or find aerial images online either, so their video mainly showed black and white photos of the school's original buildings, along with video footage of the campus now, which they shot on their phones as they drove around. Rather than focusing on the transformation of the landscape from Indian territory to settler-colonial outpost to a patch of woods yards downstream from where Thoreau took his canoe out of the Merrimack, they covered the history of the institution since the 1930s, praising its expanding programs, enrollment, and glassy new buildings. When I asked the students why they had focused so much on the school's history rather than the land's, they said they didn't want to "harsh on" the institution, so they focused instead on depicting their warm gratitude for their alma mater. Creating the video admittedly took them many hours—editing footage, putting in text, music, etc.—likely more time than other students spent researching and writing their papers—and the video's voiceover was certainly charming, as their narrative wove references to class readings into their bittersweet farewell to college. When they showed it in class, there was hearty applause and plenty of questions and comments.

The video, then, did not serve the environmental aims I had envisioned and would not provide a model for future class assignments. It may have been too much to ask these students to disentangle their feelings of attachment to people from those of place. And as with most first versions of assignments, I could have scaffolded the project much better and also modified my expectations. Such a project might work better if the whole class collaborates and contributes to it. If I get to offer the course after COVID-19, we could take field trips to the Historical Society and local museums so students could do research, offline, for photos, paintings, drawings, or text depicting local landscapes centuries ago, post those to the evolving website, and write original reflections on the changes they see. Involving the whole class could help students see how their own Nature Log photos and descriptions might become useful for others in the future, as Thoreau's local observations have proven so useful to naturalists.

Is an assignment renewable if it serves audiences and purposes one didn't intend, and veers from the subject of origin? According to Seraphin et al.'s schema, a project might be a "valuable learning exercise," but if it doesn't generate future teaching tools (92), it still falls within the realm of disposable assignments. I am quite sure that this video was "meaningful" for the students, however, as it checked off many of the criteria Eodice et al. and Anderson et al. describe. The students told me they enjoyed collaborating on the narration and filming, felt a sense of agency and creativity, and felt personal connections to their past and future identities: the film's narration closed with a meditation on how much they had learned and grown up in their time on campus.

For all the apparent openness of open-education, renewable assignments, I also wonder if writing that is truly usable for future audiences generally comes from elite institutions, or at least from upper-level students in a given major. More polished writing is more useful than rough writing. Where I teach, I can't assume that first or second-year students can write consistently correct sentences. Certainly, some students can, but it's hardly a given. Some years ago, I ran my eco-composition course as a community-engaged learning (CEL) course with third graders from a local school where 95% of students qualify for the National School Lunch program. We brought the children to campus to test water quality, have pizza, and help plant a rain garden for phytoremediation (using plants that absorb toxins). My writing class wrote signage for the rain gardens and a children's book to give to the kids, featuring the little ones as earth heroes, with text and photos of them in action. The semester ended and my students completed the book, but I needed to heavily edit it for grammar, spelling, and style to make it presentable for the 3rd graders. I haven't attempted that sort of project again, partly because the students did not seem to find it meaningful or useful, and partly because it demanded too much extra work from me past the semester. When I read about renewable assignments, then, I look to see whether the project is truly doable for the first and second-year students that I teach. While my students can do many projects well, only a few can produce the kind of polished, substantial writing that would be useful to future students or outside organizations. On the other hand, our junior and senior English majors are motivated and talented writers, and my colleagues have enlisted their skills for various digital annotation projects and community-engaged learning courses with fine results.

Renewable assignments focus on usable products of learning; but what we hope has the most lasting meaning in a literature course is, of course, the literature. In the Nature Writers course, when we read Elizabeth Kolbert on the Sixth Extinction, I hope it convinces students of the importance of seeing, recording, and telling stories about the natural world right now, in multiple media. When we read selections from David Quammen's writings on zoonotic diseases to understand how our treatment of wildlife has contributed to COVID-19, SARS, and pandemics past and to come, I hope they'll rebut the cranky uncle who insists the virus was concocted in a diabolical Chinese plot. As we read about how people have turned to nature during lockdown, overtaxing already beleaguered public lands, I'll suggest the need for much more public space in every community, and perhaps we'll write letters to legislators or town boards about investing in public land. I hope from *Walden* they can absorb a more positive view of their unchosen solitude, and of the soul-benefits of time spent wandering in natural surroundings, with a faith in the potential for change and growth.

Bibliography

Anderson, Paul, et al. "How Writing Contributes to Learning: New Findings from a National Study and Their Local Application." *Peer Review*, vol. 19, no. 1, 2017, pp.

4–8. https://ezproxy.snhu.edu/login?url=https://search.ebscohost.com/login. aspx?direct=true&db=mlf&AN=EIS123362130&site=eds-live&scope=site

Anderson, Paul, et al. "How to Create High-Impact Writing Assignments That Enhance Learning and Development and Reinvigorate WAC/WID Programs: What Almost 72,000 Undergraduates Taught Us." *Across the Disciplines: Interdisciplinary Perspectives on Language, Learning, and Academic Writing*, no. [Supplement 4], 2016. https://wac.colostate.edu/atd/hip/andersonetal2016.cfm

"Climate Change in Maine." Bates College. https://arcg.is/1iib4X

Cronon, William. American Environmental History 460 course website. Univ. of Wisconsin-Madison. http://williamcronon.net/courses/460/460_syllabus_fall_2020.html

Dobrin, Sidney. *Saving Place: An Ecocomposition Reader*. Boston: McGraw-Hill. 2005.

Eodice, Michele, et al. "The Power of Personal Connection for Undergraduate Student Writers." *Research in the Teaching of English*, vol. 53, no. 4, May 2019, pp. 320–339. https://ezproxy.snhu.edu/login?url=https://search.ebscohost.com/login.aspx?direct=true&db=edo&AN=136931156&site=eds-live&scope=site

Eodice, Michele, Anne Ellen Geller, and Neal Lerner. *The Meaningful Writing Project: Learning, Teaching, and Writing in Higher Education*. Logan: Utah State UP, 2016.

Forest Hill Cemetery: A Guide: A Romantic Landscape in Madison, Wisconsin. William Cronon's Environmental Studies 922. Nelson Institute/ Center for Culture, History, and Environment (CHE). Univ. of Wisconsin-Madison, 2015. http://foresthill.williamcronon.net/about-this-site/

Hendricks, Christina. "Renewable Assignments: Student work adding value to the world." Flexible Learning, Univ of British Columbia. 15 Oct 2015. Retrieved Dec 2020. http://flexible.learning.ubc.ca/news-events/renewable-assignments-student-work-adding-value-to-the-world/

Leslie, Claire Walker & Charles E. Roth. "Nature Journaling with School Groups" in Christian McEwen & Mark Statman, eds. *The Alphabet of the Trees: A Guide to Nature Writing*. New York: Teachers &Writers Collaborative, 2000: 93-9.

The Reader's Thoreau. Digital Thoreau. 2020. www.commons.digitalthoreau.org

Rush, Elizabeth. "Climate Change and the Stories We Tell: The Making of a Collaborative Digital Archive in Rural Maine." *PUBLIC: A Journal of Imagining America*. (Syracuse Univ.) Digital Engagements; Or the Virtual Gets Real. 4.2 https://public.imaginingamerica.org/blog/article/climate-change-and-the-stories-we-tell-the-making-of-a-collaborative-digital-archive-in-rural-maine/

Seraphin, Sally B., J. Alex Grizzell, Anastasia Kerr-German, Marjorie A. Perkins, Patrick R. Grzanka, and Erin Hardin. "A Conceptual Framework for Non-Disposable Assignments: Inspiring Implementation, Innovation, and Research." *Psychology Learning and Teaching*, vol. 18, no. 1, Mar. 2019, pp. 84–97. http://dx.doi.org.ezproxy.snhu.edu/10.1177/1475725718811711

Snyder, Gary. "The Place, The Region, and the Commons." in *The Practice of the Wild*. Wash DC: Shoemaker & Hoard, 2004. (First pub 1990): 27-51.

Teaching Resource Database. ASLE (Association for the Study of Literature and the Environment). https://www.asle.org/teach/teaching-resources-database.

Wiley, David. "What is Open Pedagogy?" *Iterating Toward Openness: Open Content.* OpenContent.org. 21 Oct 2013. https://opencontent.org/blog/archives/2975

Other Recommended Environmental Literature Syllabi with innovative and digital assignments

Cohen, Jeffrey. Literature and the Environment. George Washington University: https://www.asle.org/wp-content/uploads/gravity_forms/7-b27bad5e76c0dbac55412fa5caf472d8/2019/09/Lit-and-Enviro.pdf

Gould, Dr. Amanda Starling. Global Environmental Humanities. Duke University: https://sites.duke.edu/lit290s-1_02_s2017/

Chapter 6

Renewable Assignments and the Integrity of Intellectual Work

James M. Skidmore
University of Waterloo

Abstract

According to open pedagogy principles, "adding to the archive" also means relinquishing property rights. James M. Skidmore (University of Waterloo) in "Renewable Assignments and the Integrity of Intellectual Work" examines this tension: renewable assignments should generate openly licensed artifacts that can be modified by future users, but does renewability trump integrity of argument or interpretation? He wrestles with this issue by looking at a course and its open textbook, *Truth – Reconciliation – Story*. Part of the Cultural Identities program at the University of Waterloo, the course explores the role fiction plays in societal reckoning with large-scale human rights atrocities. Course assignments, such as edited contributions to the "Reader Voices" sections of the textbook, allow students to become part of the teaching process by contributing to the analysis of the novels in the course. Claiming that derivatives of these commentaries would lessen their meaningfulness by weakening their intellectual integrity, Skidmore argues for a revised definition of renewable assignments.

Keywords: Open Educational Resources, Creative Commons licensing, Truth and Reconciliation Commission of Canada, literature and human rights

***

At the contemporary university, we think of teaching and research as two separate and distinct activities. Academics are assessed and promoted on their abilities in each sphere, though the research often carries greater weight than the pedagogy. For students, however, learning (the other side of the teaching coin) and research are not really that separate. The average student comes to university expecting to be taught, and is perhaps surprised, and often stymied, when they realize that learning at university can be more independent than what they are accustomed to. In many courses they will study what they are told to study (their textbooks, readings, experiments, etc.), but they will also confront situations where they are set adrift to learn on their own, independently. To do that, they must consider the information before them, consult other information as well as their previous knowledge, and come to their own conclusions, tentative though they may be.

A university education can therefore be seen as an endeavour in which students transition from being learners to being independent learners, researchers of a sort. These efforts can be hindered, however, by the systematic structure of our educational enterprises. Students have been socialized into perceiving learning as a series of rewarded tasks. They do not write the essay or take the exam in order to establish their understanding of a particular topic or to demonstrate their skill in a particular area. Rather, they do so for a very particular purpose: to get a grade, and on the basis of that grade they (and their instructors) assess how much progress they have made (or not made, as the case may be).

This chapter is not the place to discuss the merits of or problems associated with grades and grading. Suffice it to say, however, that grades and grading infuse education with a transactional element. It becomes difficult for students at university, after years of tutelage in this system, to pursue interests without a transactional perspective. Learning for the sake of learning is less common than we might wish, especially within the confines of courses governed by the custom of assessing all learning with the help of grades.

The nature of transactional education should give us pause, however. Research in its purest form is not transactional. We develop an interest in a topic, and as we become more familiar with it, we bump up against a problem or a question to which we apply previous knowledge and/or seek out new knowledge in the hope of resolving the issue before us, and then we share our insights, takeaways, and other arguments with others. That is what research is all about: we ponder, investigate, communicate; we argue a point that provides insight. And this is essentially what we want our students to learn during their time in our classrooms.

In the context of a course, however, replicating this whole process is difficult, if not next to impossible. There are numerous constraints - chief among them time and lack of previous knowledge of the subject matter - that conspire with the above-mentioned socialization into a dependency model of learning that will limit the ability of most students to participate in research in its purer forms.

Our goal as educators at universities and colleges really should be to occasion a more organic approach to education that impresses upon students the desire to attain the independence needed to grow intellectually, to develop a curiosity about the complexities of the world and human existence, and equip them with the knowledge and skills needed to satisfy that curiosity. Yet if we continue to organize and teach courses according to how our own courses were organized and taught when we were students, there is a chance that we will perpetuate the socialization that fosters dependence as opposed to independence.

The sustainable education envisioned here, and which is more fully explained below, grows out of the fundamental desire to see students become part of the intellectual conversations that animate academic life. Instructors thrive on intellectual exchange, and it is only natural that we would want students to enjoy the same. We put the effort into university teaching not so that students will get the answer and move on, but so that they will learn how to participate in the intellectual work and conversations through which knowledge emerges. In their famous 1976 article "On Qualitative Differences in Learning," F. Marton and R. Säljö looked at the quality of learning as opposed to the quantity of learning, the "what" as opposed to the "how much." They discovered different levels of content processing, ranging from "surface" to "deep" learning. And it is to the depths of learning that we want our students to dive, for it is there that they will discover the meaningful ideas and skills that will sustain them in their lives.

Much of what I have mentioned here – meaningful learning, developing communication skills, engaging deeply with content – will remind you of the essay typically assigned for academic purposes. The rationale for assigning essays at university generally has three components, succinctly outlined by Maureen Fitzgerald:

> Essay writing is an important part of studying for a degree for three reasons:
>
> (1) It increases understanding and helps the process of learning because it pushes you, amongst other things, to clarify and sort out ideas and information, to analyse source material and to exercise critical judgement.
>
> (2) It develops writing skills such as the ability to structure an argument and a capacity to write lucidly, coherently and persuasively.
>
> (3) It enables your tutors to assess and provide feedback on your progress. (Fitzgerald 379)

Reason three speaks to the essay's role in assessment, reason two to its role in developing skills, and reason one to the role essays play in deep learning. If the essay really does perform the service of increasing understanding and helping students acquire analytical and critical judgement skills, as Fitzgerald argues it does, why would we want to go beyond the essay? Isn't the essay doing the heavy lifting of university learning? Is it not more prudent to leave well enough alone?

This is where David Wiley comes in. In the early 2010s Wiley, known for his pioneering contributions to the development of open educational resources

(OER), coined the term "disposable assignments" in his blog. It had occurred to him that instructors and learners together were spending millions of hours each year on producing and grading assignments that in the end would have very little meaning beyond their immediate purpose; they were disposable and would just end up being thrown away once their usefulness had run its course: "These are assignments that students complain about doing and faculty complain about grading. They're assignments that add no value to the world – after a student spends three hours creating it, a teacher spends 30 minutes grading it, and then the student throws it away. Not only do these assignments add no value to the world, they actually suck value out of the world" ("What is Open Pedagogy?").

Wiley is not referring specifically or only to essays, but we know that in the literature classroom, essays would be the prime contender for the disposable category. In the traditional approach, the learner addresses a topic in written form, which is then read, commented on, and graded by the instructor or teaching assistant. The essay is returned to the student, who might keep it or trash it. No one outside this pair is privy to what the essay contains; course essays or term papers are private communications between learner and instructor.

Wiley's criticism of the disposable assignment centres on what Wiley and Hilton call "a missed opportunity" (Wiley and Hilton 137). It's not that "these kinds of assignments cannot result in powerful student learning for that student in that context," it is simply a shame that "millions of hours of work are done, graded, and thrown away each year" (Wiley and Hilton 136-37).

We will get to Wiley's counterproposal – renewable assignments – in a moment, but first let us focus on his argument against the disposable assignment. Wiley (and Hilton) raises a fundamental question: if assignments like essays can "result in powerful student learning," why are they so quickly disposed of by the learner? Why do they have no value for the learner, and by extension for the instructor? We recognize that this is a generalization; it will not apply to every student in every learning context. But it is a contention derived from observed experience, and even though it may not stand the test of a rigorous application of the scientific method to prove its claims, the generalization resonates with many, including the editors and authors in this anthology that you are reading.

Even so, it is troubling to think that the learner does not value significant learning experiences. At another point in his original post about the disposable assignment, Wiley wonders: "What if we changed these 'disposable assignments' into activities which actually added value to the world? Then students and faculty might feel different about the time and effort they invested in them" ("What is Open Pedagogy?"). The implication is that important learning experiences that deepen a student's knowledge might nevertheless not add value to the world. It is hard for me to believe that Wiley intends to claim that learning does not enrich human existence. But it is clear that he wants something more for the learning experiences. That learning, or at least the assessment of learning, might be thought of as a waste of time – the crudest expression of the point Wiley is making – speaks to the broader issue I broached at the beginning of this chapter, namely the transactional nature that infuses so much of contemporary higher education. Essays can facilitate significant learning, but if students are accustomed to expecting learning to be reduced to transactions (an essay in exchange for a grade), once the transaction is complete and you have the grade, there is probably no good reason to hold on to the receipt (the essay itself). Wiley's description of the disposable assignment is never put in these terms, but the effects he describes align with the notion that the expectations informing our educational processes are weakening those processes.

Wiley proposes a remedy to the disposability of learning: renewable assignments, "assignments which both support an individual student's learning and result in new or improved open educational resources that provide a lasting benefit to the broader community of learners" (Wiley and Hilton 137). Assignments will have value if they teach the student something *and* if they are made freely available to support the learning of others.

It is no surprise that Wiley, one of the world leaders in open education, is promoting the open educational perspective with renewable assignments. In the Wiley and Hilton article that gives the fullest explanation of Wiley's conception of renewable assignments, they occupy one pole – the good pole – in a spectrum of assessment practices. Four types of assignments are identified, as seen in this table from the article:

Figure 6.1: Criteria Distinguishing Different Kinds of Assignments

	Student creates an artifact	The artifact has value beyond supporting its creator's learning	The artifact is made public	The artifact is openly licensed
Disposable assignments	X			
Authentic assignments	X	X		
Constructionist assignments	X	X	X	
Renewable assignments	X	X	X	X

From Wiley and Hilton, "Defining OER-Enabled Pedagogy."

Renewable assignments can do it all: provide an artifact for assessment of student progress, but one which does more than just summarize a student's learning. The renewable assignment places a student into real or realistic situations (the chief characteristic of authentic assignments), is publicly displayed (the chief characteristic of constructionist assignments), and is licensed for others to use in an open manner (the chief characteristic of renewable assignments). It is not a private affair between student and instructor, but rather a public display of learning that renews itself through uptake by other learners. Wiley writes that "the most powerful part of renewable assignments is the idea that everyone wants their work to matter" (Wiley, "Toward Renewable Assessments"): students will feel their work matters if it is authentic, public, and helps others learn, too.

Giving meaning to student learning: it is hard to find fault with that. Renewable assignments appeal to instructors for many reasons – their connections to authenticity and their emphasis on process are two factors that stand out – but imbuing a learning task with significance must be chief among them. If you are an instructor who is already sold on the promise of open educational resources, "the simple and powerful idea that the world's knowledge is a public good and that technology in general and the World Wide Web in particular provide an extraordinary opportunity for everyone to share, use, and reuse that knowledge" (Smith and Casserly 10), you will be immediately drawn to renewable assignments and their additional promise of learning artifacts that can engage learners in ways not possible with more traditional assessment practices.

Any pedagogical approach will have its downsides, however. No method exists that can meet all the needs of all learners and all instructors. The contexts of teaching and learning are multifaceted and intersectional; the most we can hope for is to find something that sits well within most of the contexts in which we are working. Wiley and Horton do not speak to this issue exactly when they ask if there are "any drawbacks (real or perceived) that are voiced by students or faculty that participate in OER-enabled pedagogy" (144). Their agenda is to bring OER to the people; all other issues take a back seat to that objective. For our purposes here it is more fruitful to pose this question with specific regard to renewable assignments. There are indeed drawbacks, and though none of them are deal-breakers, it only makes scholarly sense to enumerate them and consider how well they support the idealized notion of education outlined at the beginning of this chapter.

Renewable assignments are first and foremost assignments: tasks assigned to students, the successful performance of which will earn them a grade in their course. As such they are part of the transactional education system that creates obstacles for intellectual growth. An advantage of the renewable assignment is that its participation in open educational practices has the potential of subverting the transactional paradigm, but for that to happen, the instructor assigning the task must also be willing to challenge the framework or even work outside it. The most recent development in this regard, ungrading, envisions course tasks and assignments, and if possible courses themselves, without grades. Renewable assignments, with their authentic credentials built in, seem especially well suited to such pioneering practices, but they can also be used within the transactional system, a sort of centrist, middle-of-the-road solution to the problem of student disengagement.

Renewable assignments, like more traditional assignments, also have a deliverable, in Wiley and Hilton's terms an artifact produced by the student. One of the main differences between open educational resources and open educational practices is that the former focus on the product of learning (or that which demonstrates learning), the latter on the process of learning (or the skills gained in learning). While any learning task is going to be a mixture of both product and process, in open educational practice, process is privileged over product. The title of Wiley and Hilton's article "Defining OER-Enabled Pedagogy" hints at the tension between the two outcomes; long involvement in advocating the use of OER does not give way easily to the new, broader concept of OEP.

Wiley's long history of bringing OER into the educational mainstream can only be admired. His formulation of the 5 Rs – the permissions to retain, reuse, revise, remix, and redistribute content – have become the creed of open educators around the world and the yardstick against which openness of education materials is measured.

Figure 6.2: The 5Rs

Retain	• Make and own copies
Reuse	• Use in a wide range of ways
Revise	• Adapt, modify, and improve
Remix	• Combine two or more
Redistribute	• Share with others

From David Wiley, "Open Education. A Simple Introduction."

Wiley has been at pains to point out that any kind of licensing regime that inhibits the 5Rs also invalidates the openness of the materials being licensed, regardless of how free or redistributable they might be. He points out that under the Creative Commons licensing system, the most common method of indicating the permissions attached to OERs, licenses that prevent the sharing of revised or remixed content make that content ineligible for OER status:

Figure 6.3: The CC Licences & The 5R Activities

	CC BY	CC BY SA	CC BY NC	CC BY NC SA	CC BY ND	CC BY NC ND
Retain	✓	✓	✓	✓	✓	✓
Revise	✓	✓	✓	✓	✗	✗
Remix	✓	✓	✓	✓	✗	✗
Reuse	✓	✓	??	??	✓	??
Redistribute	✓	✓	??	??	✓	??

✓ Definitely Allowed   ✗ Definitely Not Allowed   ?? Possibly Allowed

From David Wiley, "OER, the 5Rs, and Creative Commons."

Wiley's chart puts forth the argument that the purest forms of open licensing are those that require attribution or attribution along with the condition that any use of the material be shared in the same manner (share alike). Cable Green from Creative Commons has illustrated the relationship between OER and Creative Commons licenses another way:

Figure 6.4: Relationship between OER and Creative Commons licenses

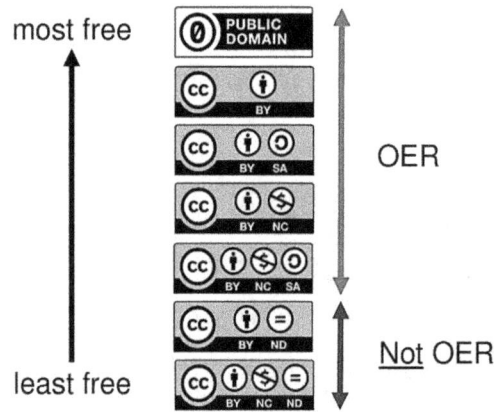

Cable Green, "Updated Keynote Slides (November, 2014)."

Green's conception of open coincides with Wiley's, though he does add the small qualification that there is a spectrum, with regard to freedom, in the Creative Commons licensing regime. But the message to the open faithful is clear: orthodox OER requires permission being granted to revise and remix the content. Open content is not on a dimmer switch; the light is either on or off – there are no shades of grey here.

Wiley's rigid definition of what constitutes OER has been widely accepted in the open education community. But it is not just in pedagogy that questions arise about the relationship between non-derivative (ND) Creative Commons licenses and open content. In the area of open access (OA) research, some scholars argue that open access research that is licensed with non-derivative conditions is by definition not open. Brigitte Vézina, Director of Policy at Creative Commons, makes this case in an article on the Creative Commons website. She cites the Budapest Open Access Initiative and its recommendations from 2002 and 2012 to point out that scholarly works are not open access if they prohibit derivatives:

> Articles published under an ND license are not considered OA, as first defined in the Budapest Open Access Initiative and in its 2012 recommendations. ND licenses overly restrict reuse of content by fellow researchers and thus curtail their opportunity to contribute to the advancement of knowledge. This is the main reason why it is inadvisable to apply ND licenses to academic publications. Although ND licenses are used for certain types of content, such as official documents that are not meant to be substantively modified, using them to forbid adaptations of academic publications flies in the face of the ethos of academic research. If anything, the ND element harms researchers. (Vézina)

Vézina is not speaking of fair use or the citation of portions of a work, all of which are permitted under a CC-ND license, but more specifically about revising or remixing the content found in scholarly publications. What she does not say, however, is that the Budapest declaration on open access makes clear the rights of the original creator to protect the integrity of their works:

> By "open access" to [peer-reviewed research literature], we mean its free availability on the public internet, permitting any users to read, download, copy, distribute, print, search, or link to the full texts of these articles, crawl them for indexing, pass them as data to software, or use them for any other lawful purpose, without financial, legal, or technical barriers other than those inseparable from gaining access to the internet itself. The only constraint on reproduction and distribution, and the only role for copyright in this domain, should be to give authors control over the integrity of their work and the right to be properly acknowledged and cited. (Budapest Open Access Initiative)

Giving authors "control over the integrity of their work" means that the last word on how a creation is to be used must rest with its creator, not its user. Yet Vézina argues that this last word should be given to the users by enabling remixing via open access:

Researchers publish to be read, to have impact, and to make the world a better place. To accomplish these important goals, researchers need to enable reuse and adaptations of their research publications and data. They also need to be able to reuse and adapt the publications and data of others. Isaac Newton, one of the most influential scientists of all time, famously declared: "If I have seen further it is by standing on the shoulders of Giants," meaning the production of new knowledge can only be achieved if researchers can rely on the ideas and publications of their peers and predecessors and revisit, reuse, and transform them, adding layer upon layer of new insights. Researchers are the ultimate remixers – OA is the ultimate way to make remixing possible.

If Vézina's argument has merit, it lies in the idealistic good she is promoting: barrier-free access to knowledge in order to enable continued scientific progress. And she is certainly not advocating theft of ideas; all Creative Commons licenses require attribution. There are nevertheless some problems with Vézina's rejection of non-derivative licenses being applied to research. No evidence is provided demonstrating that the use of non-derivative licenses, or copyright restrictions that amount to the same thing as a non-derivative license, has inhibited the ability of scholars and scientists to make use of previous research. Is application of a CC-BY-ND license really a problem in this regard?

The other issue is the preservation of the integrity of the research. Integrity here refers not to the moral value of the work, but to its completeness and wholeness. There are always going to be situations where a knowledge creator is going to wish that the integrity of their work remain whole and unchanged. For example, they might be dealing with a sensitive or highly complex issue, and they will want the points they are making to remain as they made them in order to avoid misinterpretations or misunderstandings. They may still want their thoughts and findings circulated as freely and widely as possible, and therefore choose a CC-BY-ND license. Should doing so be criticized as antithetical to open access?

Sanjaya Mishra agrees that the Budapest definition of open access referred to above "does not include remixing rights or derivative rights, as control over integrity of the work is not ceded. The context here is research articles, and very few authors of research articles would like their work to be changed" (Mishra 372). This is a good point; how would Einstein feel about his famous formula being changed to $e=mc^3$? One can counter this flippant example by pointing out that it would do no researcher any good to falsify this formula for it would lead them nowhere, both in the immediate instance and in their careers as a whole. But what about research, such as that undertaken in the humanities, where the knowledge produced comes in the form of reasoned argument? It is much easier to misconstrue, by accident or by design, the findings of humanities scholars, reliant as they are on analysis and interpretation of ideas and data (such as other texts). It makes sense that a researcher in these fields would want their ideas to be transmitted in whole in order to preserve the continuity of their claims.

To extend this point further: creators of learning materials who rely on reasoned argument and interpretation to advance student knowledge might also want to preserve the structural integrity of those works. This is a given for authors of commercial textbooks who wish to protect their intellectual property rights. But it can also apply to those academics who wish to see learning materials created by them distributed and circulated with as few obstacles as possible while at the same time maintaining the integral wholeness of those works for reasons other than financial viability, and for that reason it would make sense for them to choose a CC-BY-ND license. Mishra makes the same point; his discussion of the ND license and open access research sets up a parallel with the teaching side of the equation and OER: "What harm would it do to the OER field if ND materials were also considered OER? . . . . You can't revise or remix a work distributed with an ND licence, but that licence does allow reuse and redistribution, and one can retain a print copy of a PDF for future use. Is there no educational value in materials bearing an ND licence?" (Mishra 373)

With respect to renewable assignments, this matter becomes even thornier. According to Wiley and Hilton's definition, the artifacts produced by renewable assignments must, at a bare minimum, conform to the 5Rs of OER and involve students as (co-)creators. These student products must therefore be revisable and remixable, which in turn necessitates consideration of the implications this might have for the integrity of student work.

Returning briefly to the earlier discussion about the goals of a university education: ideally, students are part of a process in which they develop the faculties to participate in intellectual work. Being able to do so would be evidence of the "deep learning" that is often touted as a chief aim of higher education. We want students to view their time at universities and colleges less as a transaction and more as a stepping stone to a lifetime of critical inquiry and analysis. This might come naturally to some students, but for most it is a struggle to move beyond the dependent nature of learning into which they have been socialized (and into which we as instructors have socialized them) throughout their educational careers.

The examples of renewable assignments highlighted by Wiley and Hilton see students as partners in content creation, for example developing Wikipedia pages or putting together course readers and anthologies. If we are going to treat students as co-creators or co-investigators (to use the granting agency term) and not just as pupils, it is necessary for us to consider their needs and rights in any system that builds on their intellectual labours. The private nature of the disposable assignment does not require much in this regard - a grade and perhaps a few comments. But the public and open nature of the renewable assignment means more attention should be paid to how instructors can sustain the integrity of student work. An examination of my own forays into renewable assignments will help to illustrate the point I am trying to make.

When I began thinking about involving students in content creation in my courses, my first idea was to develop further an authentic task I had been assigning for many years. The online courses in German cultural studies that I have designed are very modular in nature. The 12-week courses fulfill general education requirements, are taught in English, and are open to all students at the university. They usually comprise one introductory module, eight content modules, and three study modules, with each module lasting one week. The study modules are devoted primarily to preparing MyModule, a term-long laddered project in which the students analyze the structure of the content modules in the course in order to design their own content module. Students in these courses are encouraged to follow the structure of the modules I have designed as a guide, but they have the freedom to vary from my path in order to design modules that suit the content they are researching. The MyModules are closed assignments; the students may share them with others in the course if they wish, but they are not intended for public consumption. These assignments fulfill some of the chief aims of a term paper, namely researching a topic and communicating that research, but their authenticity derives from the meta character of an assignment that gives them cause to reflect on their learning. In traditional, transactional education settings, students are usually so focused on the course requirements that they do not get a chance to consider how elements of a course or module fit together. The MyModule assignment takes a small step to remedy the situation of not being able to see the forest because of the trees. It is one thing to learn content in a course, but quite another to reflect on how one might structure and teach content, and this authentic assignment gives students a taste of that.

In 2015 the Truth and Reconciliation Commission of Canada released its report into the country's residential school scandal. The commission concluded that this system of schools, jointly organized and/or managed by the Canadian government and the United, Anglican, and Roman Catholic churches, was "an integral part of a conscious policy of cultural genocide" (Truth and Reconciliation Commission 55). In the over 100 years that the schools had been in operation before the last one closed in 1996, more than 150,000 First Nations children were removed from their families and forced to live at and attend these schools. The Commission confirmed that some 3,200 died of malnourishment, inadequate health care, and poor living conditions, though it estimated that the actual death toll might be five to ten times higher.

At the same time, the Commission issued 94 Calls to Action to the country to kickstart a reconciliation process by making amends for the grievous harm caused to First Nations peoples. Universities across the country took the spirit of these calls seriously and began working on making their institutions more inclusive for First Nations students by addressing curricular and social needs and continuing the work of the Commission to educate Canadians about the history and cultures of First Nations peoples.

As a faculty member in German studies, I began thinking about what I could do in my work to support this positive change in environment. A great deal of my teaching has addressed post-war German responses to the Holocaust, and as a result I have developed a broad understanding about how German literature has contributed to discourses surrounding memory and genocide. I thought this knowledge could be put to use in reconciliation education at the University of Waterloo. So I developed the course CI 250: Truth - Reconciliation - Story, part of a new program in Cultural Identities, to educate students about how fictional narratives portray human rights atrocities. The course is taught in English and open to all students. The calendar description of the course reads as follows:

> Modern societies have had to confront terrible histories of human rights abuses, where one group has sought to oppress and/or eliminate another because of ethnic, religious, or political differences. Truth and reconciliation commissions or similar mechanisms rely on story to express and make sense of the horrors of large-scale human rights abuses. In this course, we will examine and discuss the role of fictional narratives in contributing to the truth and reconciliation discourses of countries from around the world.

The course is organized into an introductory module introducing students to the notion of human rights and story, and then students study one or two primary works from each of the following countries: South Africa (Apartheid), Germany (the Holocaust), Canada (the residential schools scandal), the United States (slavery and segregation), and Argentina (the Dirty War of the 1970s). The novels (and occasionally films) chosen for the course have either been written during the atrocity in question (for example André Brink's 1979 novel *A Dry White Season*) or come out of a particular country's tradition of memory literature (for example Bernhard Schlink's 1995 novel *The Reader*.)

Given the course topic, and the seriousness with which I viewed the course as a contribution to Canada's own reconciliation processes, I wanted to impress upon the students the significance of the enterprise so that they might see it as a way for them to contribute to the healing necessary in our society. Courses in literature are often dismissed for their lack of connection to the "real world" (whatever that is), but in my mind nothing was more real than educating students about the responses to atrocities that had affected millions of people worldwide. It was therefore now more important to me than ever that the students engage in a meaningful manner with the content, and I needed to structure the course tasks in such a way as to minimize their transactional nature so that they would not treat the course as just another elective that they were taking to complete their degrees. And since most of the students taking the course would not be literary studies students, but rather students from diverse disciplines, my secondary goal for them was that they would leave the course with an appreciation for how fiction can crystallize the intersecting issues of history, racism, ideology, and the societal problems associated with resisting and remembering genocide and similar atrocities.

In the first iteration of the course in Winter Term 2019, I taught the course in-class, and I adapted the MyModule assignment for the course, renaming it Chapter Six. In this term-long iterative assignment, students were expected to create a module centred on a novel of their choosing that would emulate the modules they were experiencing in class. These modules provided supplementary readings to orient students to the historical and political contexts of the atrocities they were reading about in the novels. I explained to the students that I was hoping to use the class content, both my formulation of the modules plus the Chapter Six renewable assignment projects, as the basis for an open textbook that would be written after the term concluded.

I settled on the Chapter Six idea as a term-long project after considering the kinds of examples most often mentioned with renewable assignments in literary and cultural studies courses. Famous examples, all mentioned in the Wiley and Hinton article, are Wikipedia editing projects such as the Beasley-Murray "Murder and Mayhem" project as well as the anthologies of readings curated by students in courses taught Robin DeRosa and Julie Ann Ward. All three examples were excellent in their own way, but none of them really fit the context of the course I was teaching. The Wikipedia project focused on dictator novels from South America was the most analogous to Truth - Reconciliation - Story, but it required more knowledge of Wikipedia's editing practices than I had, and it would have required students to modify published articles with content that might not fit the existing structure of those articles. The anthology approach taken by DeRosa and Ward was of less interest to me as it did not foreground the interpretative skills that I wanted the students to develop and hone.

Since it was a small class, I was able to meet with the students individually three times that term to discuss the Chapter Six assignment and follow their progress. They were interested in the concept of their term project being part of an open textbook, but a number of them indicated reticence about their ability to produce a chapter that would be fit for public consumption. They felt they were outside their comfort zone, and there were a couple of reasons for this. First it became clear to the students as they progressed through the course that they had not realized the extent to which fiction is embedded in the time and place of its creation, and coming up to speed on such matters made them feel out of their depth. (For example, it will surprise many readers to learn, as it surprised me, that about a third of the students in the class had never heard of Apartheid.) The lack of prerequisites in the course was a blessing and a curse; it was good to see students from different cohorts mixing in the course, but it was clear that university experience helped more advanced students meet the challenges of the assignment with greater confidence. Very few of the students had taken university-level literature courses, and the effort to emulate the approach I was demonstrating in the course proved difficult. Finally, although I had provided students with a list of novels to give them some ideas of texts they could choose for their Chapter Six, as the students started formulating their projects, it became clear that some were relying on novels that they had studied previously in high school; the pressures of student life were preventing them from taking up the challenge to explore new work and apply the interpretive strategies being taught in the course.

The resulting Chapter Six projects demonstrated good faith efforts by most of the students, and some showed flashes of real insight into the novels and/or atrocities they were analyzing, but my overall impression was that I had asked students to take on too much. On the one hand, this was a good learning experience for them because they came to appreciate the multiple balls that instructors juggle when teaching material such as this, but on the other hand, it left both them and me feeling that they were not equipped to achieve the level of sophistication that they thought the exercise and especially the course content demanded.

In the end I decided to continue pursuing the creation of an open textbook to accompany the course, but without the Chapter Six contributions. Many of them would have required thorough editing and revision, and asking students to continue working on the projects after the course had concluded would not have been met with enthusiasm. At the same time I came to the conclusion that having students contribute discrete portions of an open text would necessitate dealing with the issue of how to maintain the integrity of their intellectual work, since one of the goals of an open textbook is to provide others with material that can be adapted to the unique circumstances of any course.

The most fundamental realization for me in this process, however, is that the Chapter Six project was failing to capture the acuity of the students' insights evident in the course itself. In our course discussions, and in the short essays they wrote for the course, the students often demonstrated a raw yet intelligent awareness of the relationship between elements of the novels, in particular with regard to character and plot development, and the larger themes of racism, truth, and reconciliation.

The second iteration of the course was scheduled for Winter Term 2021. The University of Waterloo, like all universities in Canada, had shifted to remote teaching as a result of the COVID-19 pandemic. In adapting the course for online delivery, I realized that I had an opportunity to correct some of the missteps in the first version of the course. My online teaching is largely asynchronous, and I continued that approach with CI 250 for a very specific reason. I employ discussion forums (or fora for the purists) extensively, embedding course content directly therein and having students respond to prompts and questions. Having had good success with these methods in the past, I hoped that I would be able to capture the insights that I had witnessed previously.

Primary course content remained largely similar, though two films were added to the mix. Students were required to complete three types of tasks: contributions to the discussion forums of the modules; short essays (maximum 1,000 words) focused on a specific quotation or passage of their choosing from the primary work of each module; a learning portfolio in which they submitted revised versions of their two favourite essays plus documented their course highlights and significant takeaways. None of these items was given a grade; I wanted to push the students beyond measuring their progress primarily through grades. Instead, I met with students individually three times during the course to review their progress with them, and at the last meeting we discussed and agreed on a grade for them. Two students out of 20 thought that the grade I was proposing was too low, and another two proposed grades that I thought were too low.

The results were very encouraging; the students did not disappoint. The course discussions and other submissions contained insights of the same raw quality seen in the previous offering. Though there was no renewable assignment in the course, students were made aware that I would be preparing a textbook based on the course, and that I was hoping to include their contributions by weaving in the student voice throughout the text. This meant that I would be collecting all of their input - from the discussions, from the module essays, from the learning portfolios - and working them into my text in the summer following the course. Students will be informed which pieces of their material I wish to incorporate, how I will edit them for length and clarity, and see the context in which their material will be used. At that point they will have the opportunity to grant or deny permission of use. My commentary on the works being discussed will be interspersed with student commentary and identified as such (using first name and last initial); using their comments to reflect on my approach to the subject matter and including them as needed will illustrate the intellectual dialogue that should be the hallmark of engaged, non-transactional education.

The new approach taken to CI 250 offered a kind of blend of disposable and renewable assignments. The assignments from which I am drawing the comments that will make their way into the open textbook are not exactly disposable. They are one-offs, but since no fixed grade is attached to them, the students cannot just make note of the grade and trash the assignment. The assignments are also not renewable, however, or at least not directly so because the students are not creating artifacts that are licensed and made publicly available. The students will see that their work has value beyond the immediate purposes of the course, but they will not see that during the course; our term is simply too short to make that happen. By the time the course is offered a third time, the textbook will be complete, at which point I expect to create a new type of assignment employing hypothesis to encourage the new students to discuss the instructor and student perspectives they find in the textbook. These new comments would then be incorporated in a second edition of the textbook, thereby expanding and refining the student voice within the textbook while at the same promoting the intellectual practice of discourse and commentary.

The textbook will be licensed with a CC-BY license in order to offer the greatest adaptability for other uses. I will include a note in the front matter asking anyone wishing to adapt or modify the textbook to be sensitive to the notion of intellectual integrity, especially for the content that is clearly marked as student-driven. This will not prevent the misuse of this content, but it at least alerts users familiar with OER and newcomers to its use of the importance of responsible use of material that can be highly sensitive in nature.

If I were a professor of education, I would come up with a pithy name for the modification of the renewable assignment, probably something along the lines of the blended renewable assignment. But I resist doing so in order to draw attention away from the artifact. As I have pointed out, Wiley's interest in renewable assignments is founded on his promotion of open educational resources. This is a worthy enterprise and I can only laud his efforts in this field. But the artifact produced is less important to me than the process, and intellectual growth and debate is indeed about process. The approach outlined above seeks to foster authentic student engagement with real issues of human existence. The student tasks are slightly less focused on "deliverables," I hope, and slightly more focused on interacting with ideas and forms of expression that can have significant impact on our societies. This shift in task intention aims to engage students in meaningful intellectual discourse, to help them transform their transactional learning environments into something more significant for them, their lives, and their societies. If we are serious about turning students into lifelong learners, in instilling in them sustainable analytical and interpretive skills that will help them make sense of and contribute to our world throughout their lives, we must nurture and protect the integrity of their thought.

Bibliography

Budapest Open Access Initiative | Ten Years on from the Budapest Open Access Initiative: Setting the Default to Open. https://www.budapestopenaccess initiative.org/boai-10-recommendations.

Fitzgerald, Maureen. "Why Write Essays?" *Journal of Geography in Higher Education*, vol. 18, no. 3, Jan. 1994, pp. 379–84. *DOI.org (Crossref)*, doi:10.108 0/03098269408709282.

Green, Cable. "Updated Keynote Slides (November, 2014)." Slideshare. https:// www.slideshare.net/cgreen/updated-keynote-slides-october-2014.

Marton, Ference and Roger Säljö. "On Qualitative Differences in Learning: I—Outcome and Process." *British Journal of Educational Psychology*, vol. 46, no. 1, 1976, pp. 4–11. *Wiley Online Library*, doi:10.1111/j.2044-8279.1976.tb02980.x.

Mishra, Sanjaya. "Open Educational Resources: Removing Barriers from Within." *Distance Education*, vol. 38, no. 3, Routledge, Sept. 2017, pp. 369–80. *Taylor and Francis+NEJM*, doi:10.1080/01587919.2017.1369350.

Smith, Marshall S., and Catherine M. Casserly. "The Promise of Open Educational Resources." *Change: The Magazine of Higher Learning*, vol. 38, no. 5, Routledge, Sept. 2006, pp. 8–17. *Taylor and Francis+NEJM*, doi:10.3200/CHNG.38.5.8-17.

Truth and Reconciliation Commission of Canada. *Honouring the Truth, Reconciling for the Future: Summary of the Final Report of the Truth and Reconcilliation Commission of Canada*. 2015. *OpenWorldCat*, http://epe.lac-bac.gc.ca/100/201/301/weekly_acquisition_lists/2015/w15-24-FE.html/collections/collection_2015/trc/IR4-7-2015-eng.pdf.

Vézina, Brigitte. "Why Sharing Academic Publications Under 'No Derivatives' Licenses Is Misguided." *Creative Commons*, 21 Apr. 2020, https://creative commons.org/2020/04/21/academic-publications-under-no-derivatives-licenses-is-misguided/.

Wiley, David. "OER, the 5Rs, and Creative Commons." https://docs.google.com/presentation/d/15DhTr6A5i6PYWtUriyvxGJYCriobgm_BxvxdL2yoI9g/htmlp resent

———. "Open Education. A Simple Introduction." Slideshare. https://www.slideshare.net/opencontent/open-education-a-simple-introduction.

———. "Toward Renewable Assessments." *Iterating toward Openness*, 7 July 2016. *opencontent.org*, https://opencontent.org/blog/archives/4691.

———. "What Is Open Pedagogy?" Improving Learning. https://opencontent.org/blog/archives/2975.

Wiley, David, and John Levi Hilton, III. "Defining OER-Enabled Pedagogy." *The International Review of Research in Open and Distributed Learning*, vol. 19, no. 4, Sept. 2018. 134-46. *www.irrodl.org*, doi:10.19173/irrodl.v19i4.3601.

Chapter 7
Learning Outcomes of Non-disposable Assignments: An Approach to Measuring the Results

Kerry Kautzman
Alfred University

Abstract

One of the challenges with nontraditional assignments is in fact determining how successful they are. While we may intuitively or anecdotally recognize increased engagement, Kerry Kautzman (Alfred University) in "Learning Outcomes of Non-disposable Assignments" demonstrates an approach to measuring the results. She focuses on two different kinds of renewable assignments: a critical edition to be submitted to an OER anthology of literature offering in-depth study of a canonical text and its socio-historical context, and a blog created by international-domestic student pairs exploring the developing of intercultural competency. Both assignments are writing-intensive, collaborative, multi-step projects, and both result in a digital product available both for the students' own future use and for assessment purposes. Kautzman models how to analyze the effectiveness of these assignments using rubrics that describe learning outcomes associated with traditional disposable assignments.

Keywords: learning outcomes assessment, open pedagogy, Open Educational Resources, collaborative assignments, language instruction, Spanish literature

***

To work in collaboration with a learning community toward a tangible positive output anchors my own teaching and scholarship. Given that thriving alone in the ivory tower is anathema personally, I value designing with colleagues both courses and projects that foster a sense of cohort among students while they require students to demonstrate their thinking through a variety of products. The collaborative process is one that inspires my own curiosity and love of learning. The projects reviewed here as alternative assignments to the traditional research paper reflect this approach, and each were created with respected colleagues.[1] Though the writing process of the traditional research paper can include collaborative peer review as well as the feedback and revision loop between the student and faculty member, ultimately the research paper results from one student scholar's thinking and writing. Therefore, my preference for assignment and project designs has expanded in order to center learning in community while continuing to demonstrate achievement of the same or similar learning outcomes achieved by the research paper. Nondisposable assignments (NDAs), defined as assignments that add value to the world, are a type of constructive learning that meet this objective (Wiley, et al.). As such, NDAs are applicable to a variety of scholarly and pedagogical approaches, such as the public humanities, service learning, the digital humanities, and open pedagogy, that all reflect my core principles.

Measuring the results in order to assess achievement of the learning outcomes of a nondisposable assignment contributes to existing empirical knowledge regarding the meaningful learning that occurs in a course that asks students to acquire skills not limited to those of the traditional paper. As I assess, my purpose is to evaluate to what extent the learning objectives have been met, with the explicit goal of improving course and assignment design for future use. This evaluation is not referring to the grades earned by students, but instead focuses on the merit of an assignment or course. Assessment is only as useful as it improves the student experience, faculty performance or satisfaction, and/or the rigor of an academic program. The assessment process establishes an iterative cycle of reflection about my teaching practice. I maintain my focus at the course and assignment levels of assessment but recognize alignment with macro-vision of assessment proposing to assure that both students and society are "well-served" by higher education ("Standards"). Though David Wiley states fairly in my case that, as a faculty member in a Modern Languages program with expertise in literature of Spain, I have "no training in psychometrics," I am not willing to populate Alfred's Spanish program with courses and assignments "never evaluated in terms of the reliability and validity of their results" (Wiley, "Toward"). Therefore, I depend on the resources created by better trained and trusted experts. Rubrics, such as those adapted from the Intercultural Communication Institute and American Association of Colleges & Universities (AAC&U), allow me to streamline this deliberate reflective cycle. My commitment to particular types of assignments and their

---

[1] These colleagues include, among others, Dr. Vicky Westacott, Dr. Cecilia Beach, Dr. Erin Redmond, Carla Allende, Isabel García Lavandero, Meghanne Frievald, Gary Roberts, Samantha Dannick, and Carter Adams from Alfred University, as well as Dr. Brenda García Portillo and Gretel Werner from the *Universidad de Monterrey*, México.

assessments reflects broader innovations in theory and practice of teaching and scholarship in the Liberal Arts. As an innovation, open education "is that set of teaching and learning practices only possible in the context of the free access and the [retain, reuse, revise, remix, and redistribute] permissions characteristic of open educational resources" (Wiley, "What"). Open Education, Open Educational Resources (OERs), and NDAs challenge the reified hierarchy of academia and create a space for agency in which all stakeholders share knowledge transparently. Given that shared accountability among team members for a collaboratively created product appeals to my teaching and scholarly approaches and that one of the tools of open education is the non-disposable assignment, I appreciate that these assignments decenter the faculty member as the expert judge and jury member and offer the students the leadership roles that reward initiative, organization, and follow-through. Qualities I heartily wish only to see in ascendence.

The public humanities engage an inclusive audience that connects university faculty, staff, and students with diverse communities beyond academia. Public humanities' community engagement extends the creation, benefits, and results of scholarship in the humanities to its inclusive audience by means of public events, media representation, and community collaboration. Each of these three outcomes align with the fundamental character of a non-disposable assignment. Service learning integrates community service with academic instruction and personal reflection. Service learning offers a given community the solution to a problem or a lack while it offers the individual learner first-hand experience collaborating in the design and implementation of those solutions. Again, this is a pedagogy whose outcome adds something to the world as an NDA. The digital humanities intersect digital technologies and scholarship in the humanities. The technologies support collective networks of scholars in the humanities as well as influence and effect the experience and results of the scholarship depending on the functionality of a given technology. Inasmuch as open pedagogy connects classroom instruction to external communities, requires work with an audience beyond the professor, and results in tangible benefits to learners and a wider community, it belongs in a cohort with the aforementioned teaching-researching strategies. Open pedagogy positions student learners as the creators of knowledge. Their creation of knowledge disrupts the for-profit market of texts resulting in Open Educational Resources (OERs) as well as the concept of copyright as a private individual license while it offers the knowledge created by the learners to a broader community. As promoted by Wiley, when students create the knowledge in an open pedagogy context, they and all future users or creators be "retain the right to make, own, and control copies of the content" (Wiley, "What"). The work, be it a text, a public event, a media campaign, or collaborative project, belongs to the public.

The students as creators of knowledge can reuse "the content in a wide range of ways" (Wiley, "What").

To defend their use as alternatives to the traditional research paper, NDAs should satisfy four learning objectives that, as faculty in a Spanish program, appear on nearly all my syllabi, including proficient oral and written communication, critical reasoning and analysis, information literacy, and intercultural competency. They can be labeled as course learning objectives or student learning outcomes. Ideally, standard or typical academic tasks confirm student learning and comply with expectations of measurability of these skills. For example, the traditional research paper requires three of the aforementioned skills, though it does not address intercultural competency. Beyond my pedagogical philosophy, pragmatic concerns, such as the ability to purchase papers online, lead me to question the efficacy of the research paper as the best task to practice the aforementioned skills, especially as courses aim to improve students' intercultural competency. Furthermore, in the case of the traditional writing assignment, there is the contradiction between my exhortations to students about being life-long learners with useful tools to carry forward into the future and the truth that post-university life does not ask for research papers per se, but reasoned thinking and clarity of expression. The affective experience of the students presents the most important challenge to the reign of the research paper inasmuch as I have found it to inspire intellectual curiosity within a narrow student demographic that does not represent the interests and needs of a broad range of students at my institution, hence the divide between disposable assignments exemplified by the research paper and nondisposable assignments that are valuable beyond their assessable measurability because they exist outside the course (both in space and in time) within the greater community (Chen). Fostering this love of learning or intellectual curiosity is the first and foundational objective of my interactions with students. David Wiley and many Open Education colleagues and mentors have expressed these concerns with greater acuity than I might here.

For this essay I review assignments and assessments from three courses that include non-disposable assignments (NDAs) and are in the Spanish program, while the fourth course is in the Global Studies program. Two of the courses are introductory level courses of Alfred's General Education program and two are upper-level courses of the Spanish program. Though learning goals are particular to each, the four courses in which students participated in NDAs share general, overarching learning outcomes and are typical of many language and literature courses in the Liberal Arts. These outcomes work in relation to one another and are scaffolded to provide the baseline skill necessary for the more advanced goal to be achieved. The tasks of these courses ask students to develop their communication skills in order to participate in multilingual communities, to acquire knowledge of their own and others' cultures and their socio-historical development in order to be interculturally competent, and finally to develop information literacy in order to demonstrate critical reasoning and analytical skills. The learning outcomes mentioned here sync with institutional outcomes as well as national benchmarks established by organizations such as Modern Languages Association (MLA), American Council on the Teaching of Foreign Languages (ACTFL), the aforementioned Intercultural Communication Institute, and AACU.

More significant to pedagogy, all four tasks were collaborative with an audience beyond the course professor and could exist physically and temporally beyond the classes taught. The beginning level courses complete a series of proficiency-building, community-building and/or cultural tasks that culminated in a final reflective essay. Examples of tasks include watching an assigned movie together and comparing responses, choosing a community event together and discussing it, a mutual structured interview, and a communal dinner. Only the final reflective essay was done individually. It is the final reflective essay that was assessed. To complete the digital or virtual student-to-student exchange with the Universidad de Monterrey, Mexico, in Introductory Spanish, we added a zero-credit lab hour to the four-credit course and named the NDA "Intercambio virtual" or Virtual Exchange. Two Alfred Spanish professors, Alfred Fulbright teaching assistants from the Institute of International Education (IIE), and two Monterrey faculty and staff members coordinated the exchange with support from Alfred's Instructional Technology Services (ITS). The French program organized a parallel exchange. For the Introduction to Global Studies collaboration with two classes in the English as a Second Languages (ESL) program, English Skills for Multilingual Speakers and Writing I for nonnative speakers, we named the non-disposable assignment "International Education Experience" but did not formally add any additional time to the course. In this case, student pairs completed the series of tasks and the final reflective essay outside the classroom as homework. The faculty of the two Alfred courses, Global Studies and English as a Second Language, coordinated this exchange with assistance from a peer-leader, a junior hired to assist first-year students with their adjustment to college. Students in both exchange projects completed a series of asynchronous tasks that culminated in a final reflective essay. We modified the Intercultural Knowledge and Competence VALUE rubric from the AAC&U for assessment of the exchanges based on the final reflective essays (Rhodes). Alfred University's Division of Modern Language's upper-level Spanish course Literary Theory Seminar depended in two consecutive years on Dr. Julie A Ward's *Antología abierta de literatura hispana*, an OER from the Rebus Community housed on PressBooks as they created a critical edition.

The work samples produced by these nondisposable assignments were evaluated against standard rubrics (appendices A and B). Though we applied intercultural competency and written communication assessment rubrics, we might have chosen an integrated learning rubric or a rubric from Modern Languages program assessment. Assessing a course or assignment is not grading an assignment, and I provide a typical rubric that I use for grading as a contrast (Appendix C). Results must be characterized as statistically insignificant. The results were not reached through hypothesis testing, normal distribution, nor p value. The two Literary Theory Seminars included a total of seven students in a four/three split of the spring 2019 and 2020 semesters. The Introductory Spanish exchange included my section of 22 students as well as the 63 students of colleagues' sections. The Introduction to Global Studies assignment has been completed once during the fall of 2020 by sixteen students. It is unclear when I will have another opportunity to teach the course.

For the *Intercambio virtual* of the Introductory Spanish I classes, a formal exchange was established with colleagues at the Universidad de Monterrey, Mexico. The Alfred French program initiated a similar exchange in the same semester. The concept was to pair one Alfred Introductory Spanish I student with one Monterrey returning study abroad student. By contrast the French program attempted the exchange at the intermediate level as well. Each Alfred/Monterrey pair would complete a weekly lesson together over the course of fourteen weeks. Alfred students finished the semester with a final reflective essay. The Alfred faculty of the Spanish program created the weekly lessons, the evaluations of student performance, and the assessment of results for future revisions. The lessons were cultural in focus and designed in Spanish. Though both Monterrey and Alfred have strong engineering programs, in general there were great differences in the two student demographics. For example, none of the Alfred Spanish I students had studied abroad while all of the Monterrey students had for as much as a year. Most of the Alfred students were in the Liberal Arts while many Monterrey students were in STEM fields. The exchange occurred during the fall of 2014 and 2015 but was discontinued as a result of an imbalance of participants. The Alfred group doubled the Monterrey group in size (85/48 in 2014) which placed undue pressure on the Monterrey students to work with two and, on occasion, three Alfred students while it prevented the Alfred students from establishing a connection with just one Monterrey student. Nearly all communication occurred via email, Facebook, and Skype. Significantly, the Alfred students reported discomfort with the technology use required for the exchange. This would necessarily increase their affective filter or anxiety. During the intervening years, technology has continued to develop and, obviously, would change the design of the exchange in practical terms if it were attempted in the future. Of the eighty-five Alfred participants, sixty-one completed self-assessments which provide some interesting indications that can be used to improve the design of the activities. Forty percent of the self-reporting described communicating with Monterrey partners mostly in English. This was predicted to be higher given the novice language level of the Alfred students and the interest in the study abroad students to use a language other than their dominant language. A quarter of the participants reported using only Spanish in a given exchange. As predicted, self-reporting about a greater interest in other cultures, in study abroad, and in meeting people from other cultures skewed positive. The final reflective essay was assessed with our modified Intercultural Knowledge and Competence VALUE rubric that included five components: knowledge of cultural self-awareness, knowledge of cultural worldview frameworks, empathy, communication style, and open curiosity. In general, the results rated at a two indicating "developing competence" when the reflection

- Begins to identify own cultural assumptions, rules, biases, and judgments.
- Expresses a strong preference for own cultural rules.
- Articulates surface understanding of the social relationships and other dynamics of one's own culture in relation to another's culture.
- Demonstrates some knowledge of the values, history, patrimony, politics, economy, communication styles, or beliefs and practices of another culture.
- Distinguishes components of other perspectives.
- Responds to all situations/interactions with own cultural rules and biases.
- May begin to negotiate an understanding based on one's own communication style
- May express awareness of some of his/her misunderstandings.
- May identify some cultural differences in verbal and nonverbal communication style.
- Asks simple surface level questions about culture without suspending judgment.
- Expresses openness to interactions with those of another culture but may polarize differences into us/them distinctions
- May express preference for one's own culture

In both the Introductory Spanish and Introduction to Global Studies exchanges, students are completing General Education courses that they typically choose earlier in their academic careers. Therefore, results that indicate developing competence are appropriate and communicate the opportunity for academic programs to build courses and assignments that lead students toward increased levels of intercultural competence over the course of their academic careers. The International Education Experience had three explicit goals that were aligned with greater course, program, unit, and institutional goals and expressed within the applied rubric. Students were partnered, and the pairs had three shared activities – an interview exchange, an American event, and a shared meal – to complete. After each activity, students individually completed a reflection with a final overall reflection as a fourth written component. Since at no point did the assignment approach its initial characterization as a blog, it did not produce a public text that can be remixed or redistributed. However, as an experience, it was renewable within the Alfred community as international students and first-year Global Studies students build relationships and form a community. (Appendix D)

For the two critical editions, written in Spanish, each group chose a text from the public domain and followed guidelines established by Ward for her anthology. They prepared an introduction, the annotated text, a set of comprehension questions, and a bibliography. In multiple courses I use this anthology as a cost-free source of OER readings. Therefore, the students knew that their target audience was undergraduate students in other Spanish programs nationally. With the first cohort I strictly followed Ward's guidelines. For the second I adapted them, but with unsatisfactory results. Ward's guidelines or lesson plans cover seven class periods over ten weeks and are outlined fully in a handbook. Ward's guidelines emphasize working as a team and group accountability. Based on a comparison of the two AU scholarly editions, I am convinced that all seven (and a half) sessions/ten weeks must happen in person in the seminar. Additionally, cohort size influences the outcomes. In both sections completing this assignment there were fewer than five students. Therefore, only one text was being annotated in a given semester. This affected the selection process of a text to annotate. Peer feedback among two or more groups was impossible, which normalized the good and bad scholarly strategies in the single group of a given semester. For the students who participate, this assignment is valuable outside the classroom's space and time as a potential publication for a resume. For undergraduate students of the discipline nationally, it is valuable outside the classroom because Ward's anthology is revised and expanded and consequently more likely to be adopted for other undergraduate Spanish language literature courses.

Assessment of the critical editions included the five components of written communication: content, organization, expression, mechanics, and citation.

While the first cohort's work sample resulted in ratings of three, indicating competent written communication, the second cohort's work sample resulted in ratings of two, indicating developing competence in written communication. Competent written communication denotes that the task was accomplished with clear paragraphs and intended meaning, an organizing principle, though the citations contain errors. Language use was comprehensible. (Appendix E) In the writing sample that exhibits developing competence the appropriate task is not carried out. The paragraphs lack focus. Though meaning is generally clear because language use was competent, any organization must be deciphered. The citations contain errors. (Appendix F) As I assessed these work samples, I learned that, in both samples, students developed a different skill set than the intended proficient written communication. Instead, the samples demonstrate competence and advanced competence in the practice of close reading in a second language. In previous courses during which students wrote an analytical paper, the writing sample was extensive in word-count or pages, but the assessment results were also at the developing competency and competent levels. If I consider the amount of language output at an individual level, then I cannot argue confidently that the outcomes of the critical edition make the outcomes of the research paper. I'll need to address this and develop additional materials that help the students produce more formal and informal writing.

As a learner and an educator, I am reminded of best practices and have learned new lessons to apply in future classes. With renewable assignments completed in the hands-on workshop setting of a google doc, I am confident that my students themselves wrote the words that I use to evaluate their progress. This was also true of the reflections submitted for the intercultural exchange. My rigorous use of the multistep structure of the critical edition created by Ward for her anthology is a must (as demonstrated by the differences between the two critical editions when I tried to innovate). I cannot assume technological proficiency on the part of the students at any point. Though I have often benefitted from those who are more knowledgeable, I have to create in advance any template for a blog that I ask the students to use. We need to list which skills are acquired and to include close reading as an objective for the Literary Theory Seminar. For the International Education Experience, I would like to try to add some additional campus experiences.

Appendix A

Intercultural Knowledge & Competence Assessment Rubric
–Alfred University

Student ID number _____   Score _____

Reader's name   _____

		Advanced (4)	Competent (3)	Developing Competence (2)	Inadequate (1)
Knowledge	**Cultural self-awareness** (Obtaining knowledge of self & others)	Recognizes one's own rules, biases and judgments about one's own culture and the culture of others. Articulates insights into cultural rules and the influence of personal experiences on biases and judgments. Responds to cultural biases by assessing their impact and articulating a shift in self-description.	Recognizes new perspectives about own cultural assumptions, rules, judgments, and/or biases. Articulates the influence of one's own biases, assumptions, and/or judgments during interactions with one's own culture and the culture of others.	Begins to identify own cultural assumptions, rules, biases, and judgments. Expresses a strong preference for own cultural rules.	Demonstrates little or no awareness of one's own judgments or biases about self and others. Exhibits discomfort identifying cultural differences with others.
	Cultural worldview frameworks (Obtaining knowledge of self & others)	Articulates understanding of the complexity of elements important to another culture in relation to its history, patrimony, values, politics, economy, communication styles, or beliefs and practices. Acceptance of the existence of multiple worldviews when comparing and contrasting one's own culture and that of others	Articulates partial understanding of complex social relationships and other dynamics important to one's own culture & members of other cultures. Conflates worldviews when expressing an understanding of another culture's values, history, patrimony, politics, communication styles, economy, or beliefs and practices.	Articulates surface understanding of the social relationships and other dynamics of one's own culture in relation to another's culture. Demonstrates some knowledge of the values, history, patrimony, politics, economy, communication styles, or beliefs and practices of another culture.	Demonstrates only one worldview with little or no understanding of social relationships and or other dynamics important to one's own culture in relation to another's culture. Demonstrates no knowledge of the values, history, patrimony, politics, economy, communication styles, or beliefs and practices of another culture.

Skills	**Empathy**	Interprets intercultural experiences from the perspectives of own and more than one worldview. Demonstrates ability to act in a supportive manner that recognizes the feelings of another cultural group.	Recognizes intellectual and emotional dimensions of more than one worldview. Responds to some situations/interactions with more than one worldview in interactions.	Distinguishes components of other perspectives. Responds to all situations/interactions with own cultural rules and biases.	Views cultural experience through own cultural rules.
	Verbal & nonverbal communication style	Recognizes differences in verbal and nonverbal communication style among one's own and others' cultures. Incorporates these diverse and multiple perspectives in verbal and nonverbal communication. Negotiates and facilitates a shared and understanding among one's own and others' cultures.	Recognizes some cultural differences in verbal and nonverbal communication among cultures. May incorporate multiple perspectives when working with members of one's own and other cultures. Begins to negotiate a shared and mutual understanding due to knowledge of pragmatics and communication styles.	May begin to negotiate an understanding based on one's own communication style. May express awareness of some of his/her misunderstandings. May identify some cultural differences in verbal and nonverbal communication style.	Conveys minimal or no awareness of verbal and non-verbal communication style differences. Expresses fear and anxiety about being able to communicate with people of other cultures
Attitude	**Curiosity Openness**	Seeks and integrates experiences that broaden understanding of one's own culture and behavior and the culture and behavior of others. Initiates, engages with, and values interactions with one's own and the culture of others while assessing their impact. Asks complex questions and formulates answers that reflect multiple cultural perspectives.	Seeks opportunities to question and to broaden understanding of one's own culture and the culture of others. Begins to initiate interactions with culturally different others. Minimizes differences and asserts cultural commonalities but may avoid adaptations to another culture.	Asks simple surface level questions about culture without suspending judgment. Expresses openness to interactions with those of another culture but may polarize differences into us/them distinctions May express preference for one's own culture	Demonstrates little or no awareness of or interest in learning about one's own and others' cultures. Little or no awareness of own cultural rules, judgments, and biases.

This rubric was created using the Association of American Colleges and Universities (AAC&U) Critical Thinking VALUE Rubric. Retrieved from https://www.aacu.org/value-rubrics

Appendix B

College of Liberal Arts and Sciences Written Communication Assessment Rubric – Alfred University

Student ID number _____

Reader's name _____

	Advanced (4)	Competent (3)	Developing Competence (2)	Inadequate (1)
Content (what the writer communicates) Result:	Writer defines an appropriate task for the essay, communicates that task to the reader, and follows through with detail and precision.	Writer defines and carries out an appropriate task for the essay, though treatment may be superficial or lack detail.	Writer fails to define or carry out an appropriate task for the essay; treatment of the topic may be significantly underdeveloped or oversimplified.	Writer does not appear to fully understand the topic.
Structure/Organization (how readily the reader can follow the writer's development of ideas) Result:	Each paragraph fully develops one idea, and paragraphs flow logically in service of a clearly articulated overall purpose.	Each paragraph develops a clearly articulated idea; writer may not articulate meaningful relationships between paragraphs, but an overall organizing principle is present.	Individual paragraphs may be unfocused; their relationships to each other and to the essay's larger goal may not be obvious.	The purpose of individual paragraphs and their relationships to each other are unclear; the essay lacks an overall organizing principle.
Expression (how the writer communicates the content) Result:	Writer's prose is clear, fluid, concise, and engaging, employing varied sentence structure and precise language choices.	Writer's intended meaning is clear and sentences are generally concise, but prose lacks sophistication; sentences may not flow smoothly, and vocabulary may occasionally be imprecise.	Writer's intended meaning is generally clear. Sentences may be wordy or overwritten, and language may be repetitive or used inappropriately.	Sentences are difficult to comprehend; language may be misused, and tone may be inappropriate for academic writing.
Mechanics (grammar, punctuation, format) Result:	The essay is essentially error-free.	There may be occasional errors in grammar or punctuation, but they do not interfere with the flow of the sentences.	There may be noticeable errors in grammar or punctuation, but they do not interfere with the comprehensibility of the sentences.	Errors in grammar and punctuation are so distracting and/or confusing that sentences are difficult to follow.
Citation (intellectual property indicated) Result:	It is always possible to differentiate between the student's ideas and others'. The reader always could find the source based on information provided.	It is always possible to differentiate between the student's ideas and others'. The reader may or may not be able to find the source based on information provided.	It is generally possible to differentiate between the student's ideas and others'. The reader could not find the source based on the information provided.	It is not possible to differentiate between the student's ideas and others'. The reader could not find the source based on the information provided.

Appendix C

El criterio para la calificación del trabajo escrito

I. La comprensión:

    Casi todo es incomprensible.   1-10 %

    Por lo general es comprensible; sin embargo

        hay oraciones que necesitan interpretación.   11-19 %

    Es totalmente comprensible.   20-25% _____

II. La cohesión ([1]los borradores, [2]la introducción, 3-4 argumentos/párrafos centrales, [5]la conclusión):

    La composición es una serie de oraciones

        separadas sin sentido y sin transiciones.   1-10%

    La composición tiene algo de sentido pero

        falta lógica y fluidez de expresión.   11-19%

    La composición tiene fluidez y estilo.   20-25%_____

III. El contenido (una lectura cuidadosa / un análisis de unos ejemplos específicos):

    Contiene poca información; no ofrece

        ningún análisis ni lectura cuidadosa   1-10%

    Contiene información adecuada para el tema;

        empieza a analizar.   11-19%

    Contiene información detallada y completa,

        una lectura cuidadosa.   20-25%_____

IV. El vocabulario y la gramática:

Es inadecuado; se repite; es incorrecto;

    hay errores de significado.   1-10%

Es adecuado sin embargo contiene errores.   11-19%

Hay variedad de estructuras gramaticales

    y de vocabulario que es preciso y expresivo.   20-25%_____

                                    TOTAL: _____

Comentario:

Appendix D

In our textbook, Steger argues that globalization "applies to a set of social processes" (9). Of course, higher education is an important social process. All of you are in the process of studying for your Alfred University college degree. According to the Association of International Educators (NAFSA), more than 332,000 students from the United States studied abroad last year.[2] That is an increase from previous years and represents about 10% of college graduates. What happens to those students from Alfred University and other universities and colleges when they study abroad? Who supports them? What is their daily routine like once they arrive to their study abroad destination? One way for us to learn more is to support AU's international students who are studying abroad right here in Alfred, New York.

International Education helps us think about culture as a concept. With it, we learn about cultures around the world. It helps us learn about our own culture as well. We will define culture as the "accumulated pattern of values, beliefs, and behaviors share by an identifiable group of people with a common history and verbal and nonverbal code system" (Neulip xvii). Culture helps us know how we should behave in our daily situations. We might take appropriate behavior for granted as plain common sense. When we interact with people from other cultures, we often see that what we recognize as familiar is

---

[2] Here is NAFSA's website for those of you interested in International Education. Here is more detailed information about who from the United States is studying where in the world. https://www.nafsa.org/ https://www.nafsa.org/Policy_and_Advocacy/Policy_Resources/Policy_Trends_and_Data/Trends_in_U_S__Study_Abroad/

unfamiliar, or even inappropriate, to someone from another culture. What does it take to be interculturally competent at that moment of misrecognition? Our current activity begins to seek an answer to this question. It is important to learn how to answer this question while you all are at Alfred University. Of the eight competencies that the National Association of Colleges and Employers look for as "career readiness," you're developing at least two of them: Oral/Written Communications and Global/Intercultural Fluency.[3] Importantly, employers don't rate their new hires as always being very career ready for communication and intercultural fluency. You can stand out and highlight your openness and empathy as an advocate of international education.

Appendix E

Aunque refleja el debate unamuniano contradictorio, el prólogo de *Tres novelas ejemplares y un prólogo* (1920) tiene un estilo único. Unamuno empieza con una innovación literaria: "nívola." Es su manera de corresponder con la multitud que sabe lo básico. Unamuno escribe para comunicarse tanto con los lectores que poseen una educación extraordinaria, como tiene el mismo escritor, como con los lectores que no la poseen. Su vida está rodeada de intelectuales lo cual no es cotidiano para la persona ordinaria. En su obra, Unamuno apoya de modo explícito al hombre común. Aunque usa palabras terruñeras, sus ideas son complicadas porque através que mirar esta obra en otro modo más abstracto pero también concreto.

Appendix F

Puertos americanos

Los puertos americanos consistieron de puertos de Veracruz, Cartagena de Indias, Salvador de Bahía y Pernambuco. Los puertos de Cumana (Venezuela) y la isla del caribe como Jamaica y Barbados fueron utilizados por los holandeses y ingleses para trasladar a los esclavos negros a América (Eltis et la 2010). Los puertos de embarque funcionaron en base al sistema de "Asiento de Negro" que consistió de un asentista que le pagó a la Corona en cambio por obtener un cierto número de esclavos para llevar a América que fue determinado en base a un tiempo fijo (Cantillo 1843). El sistema de "Asiento de

---

[3] Here is the website for the National Association of Colleges and Employers and their Career Readiness list. Here are the statistics built from the feedback that employers provide about their new hires' career readiness.
https://www.naceweb.org/career-readiness/competencies/career-readiness-defined/
https://www.naceweb.org/career-readiness/competencies/employers-rate-career-competencies-new-hire-proficiency/

Negro" fue un tipo de monopolio: un monopolio sobre el comercio de esclavos desde África y las Américas (Cantillo 1843).

Bibliography

Chen, Baiyun. "Foster meaningful learning with renewable assignments." In Baiyun Chen et al. (Eds.), *Teaching Online Pedagogical Repository*. Orlando, FL, University of Central Florida Center for Distributed Learning, 2018, https://topr.online.ucf.edu/r_1h7ucljsasbkbsd/. Retrieved March 3, 2020.

Rhodes, Terrell. *Assessing outcomes and improving achievement: Tips and tools for using rubrics*. Washington, DC, Association of American Colleges and Universities, 2010.

"Standards." Middle States Commission on Higher Education, 2021. https://www.msche.org/standards/

Ward, Julie Ann, editor. *Antología abierta de literatura hispana*. 2017. https://press.rebus.community/aalh/

Ward, Julie Ann. "Critical Edition Assignment Implementation Guide." *A Guide to Making Open Textbooks with Students*. Fort Hays State U Digital Press. https://fhsu.pressbooks.pub/makingopentextbookswithstudents/chapter/teachingassignment-expand-an-open-textbook/

Ward, Julie Ann et al. "Opening up Hispanic Literature: An Open-Access Critical Edition Assignment." *InSight: A Journal of Scholarly Teaching*, v15, 2020, pp. 122-141.

Wiley, David. "Toward Renewable Assessments." Open Content, 7 July 2016, https://opencontent.org/blog/archives/4691.

———. "What is Open Pedagogy?" Open Content, 21 October 2013, https://opencontent.org/blog/archives/2975.

Wiley, David et al. "A Preliminary Exploration of the Relationships Between Student-Created OER, Sustainability, and Students' Success." *International Review of Research in Open and Distributed Learning*, vol. 18, no. 4, June 2017.

Contributors

Dr. **Allison Cummings** is a Professor of English at Southern New Hampshire University whose courses include American Literature, Genre Studies, Nature Writers, Black Literary Tradition, Poetry Writing Workshop, and composition. She has published poetry and articles on contemporary American poetry in journals such as *Passages North*, *The Literary Review*, and *Contemporary Literature*. She has also published nonfiction essays, book reviews, and articles on teaching and has edited several literary magazines.

Dr. **Francisco Delgado** is a writer and teacher based out of Queens, NY. His research focuses on Native American/Indigenous literatures and has been featured in *Memory Studies*, *The CEA Critic*, *Transmotion*, and *Teaching American Literature: Theory and Practice* and is forthcoming in *Teaching English In the Two-Year College*. His chapbook of flash fiction/prose poems, *Adolescence, Secondhand* was published by Honeysuckle Press in 2018. He is an Assistant Professor of English at Borough of Manhattan Community College, City University of New York.

Dr. **Kerry Kautzman** completed her undergraduate studies at Gannon University, majoring in International Studies before earning her Ph.D. at the University of Cincinnati in Spanish Literature. In her two decades at Alfred University, she has taught a wide range of courses in Spanish language and literatures, critical theory, Women's and Gender Studies, and Social Justice Studies. Her current research and teaching interests focus on the literature of Equatorial Guinea.

Dr. **Melissa Ryan** is a Professor of English at Alfred University specializing in American literature and Social Justice Studies. Her work has appeared in *African American Review*, *ISLE: Interdisciplinary Studies in Literature and the Environment*, *Studies in the Novel*, *ESQ: A Journal of the American Renaissance*, *ATQ: American Transcendental Quarterly*, *Studies in American Fiction*, and *American Literature*.

Dr. **James Skidmore** is Associate Professor of German and Director of the Waterloo Centre for German Studies at the University of Waterloo, Canada, specializing in contemporary German literature and culture, comparative literature, politics in literature and film, and online learning. He is the author of *The Trauma of Defeat. Ricarda Huch's Historiography during the Weimar Republic*, as well as many book chapters and scholarly articles. He has won two national and one university teaching award, and has served as an Open Education Fellow with eCampusOntario.

Aoise Stratford (MFA, PhD) is a playwright, dramaturg, and a Lecturer at Cornell University in the department of Performing and Media Arts. Her work has been staged at National Theatre London, SoloChicago (Jeff Award nomination), The New York City Fringe Festival (Time Out NY Critics Pick), Centenary Stage (Susan Glaspell Award) and The Hangar Theatre (Niedekorn award), among others. Her scholarship has been published in *Theatre Survey*, *The Journal of Dramatic Theory and Criticism*, *The Dramatist*, and *Modern Drama*. Her recent essay "Why Numbers Count: Looking at Producing More Women" appeared in *Frontiers: A Journal of Women Studies*. Recent essays on feminist writers Dorothy Hewett and Liz Lochhead are forthcoming in *The Routledge Anthology of Women's Theatre Theory and Dramatic Criticism*, and her article "Teaching Susan Glaspell's *Trifles* in the Writing Room" is forthcoming in *Susan Glaspell In Context* from Cambridge University Press.

Dr. **Akiyoshi Suzuki** is a professor of American literature and world literature at Nagasaki University, Japan. He has held positions such as guest professor at Suzhou University of Science & Technology in China, external reviewer of research proposals at the Chinese University of Hong Kong, and is now president of Katahira English Literature Society, and editor-in-chief of Japan Society of Text Study and Japan Society of Stylistics, and others. Dr. Suzuki has introduced innovative and inventive readings of literature, such as 3-D topographic reading of Haruki Murakami's fictions, resistance against identity-centrism reading of Henry Miller's fictions, and so on.

Index

A

All My Relations, 4, 5
Antología abierta de literatura hispana, ed. Julia Ward, 114
Association for the Study of Literature and the Environment (ASLE), 74

C

collaborative learning, 9, 24, 28, 50, 66, 74, 111
Creative Commons, 72, 95
Cronon, William, 75

D

Diaz, Junot, 61
Digital Humanities, 74
diversity, equity, and inclusion, ix, 14, 19, 53, 59
dramaturgy, 18

F

Fuchs, Elinor, 23
funds of knowledge, 58

H

hongaku, 42
Humanities, value of, vii

I

intercultural competence, 8, 62, 114

K

Kamo no Chōmei, 41

L

La Sorcière, Jules Michelet, 48
Lin Yutang, 36
Love Medicine, 10
Lullaby, by Leslie Marmon Silko, 62

N

Norwegian Wood, Murakami Haruki, 48

O

Of Mice and Men, 49
online teaching, 18, 49, 82, 104
Open Educational Resources (OER), viii, 72, 92, 95, 109
Orlando (play by Sarah Ruhl), 28
Ovid's *Metamorphoses*, 41

Q

Quarantine, by Rahul Mehta, 64

R

Rodriguez, Richard, 57
rubrics, 6, 25, 65, 111, 116, 118, 119

T

The Clash of Civilizations and the Remaking of World Order, 40
The Geography of Thought, Richard E. Nisbett, 35
The Great Gatsby, 44, 49
The Joy Luck Club, 63
The Meaningful Writing Project: Learning, Teaching and Writing in Higher Education, 78
The Reader's Thoreau, 74
Trifles, 23
Truth and Reconciliation Commission of Canada, 100

U

Universal Design for Learning (UDL), ix

W

Wiley, David, vii, 3, 56, 72, 91, 108

Z

Zhang Longxi, 34, 37, 45

www.ingramcontent.com/pod-product-compliance
Lightning Source LLC
Chambersburg PA
CBHW061416300426
44114CB00015B/1964